CYSA+ STUDY GUIDE
EXAM CS0-003

IT SECURITY FOR VULNERABILITY AND THREAT INTELLIGENCE ANALYSTS

4 BOOKS IN 1

BOOK 1
FOUNDATIONS OF CYBERSECURITY: A BEGINNER'S GUIDE TO CYSA+ EXAM CS0-003

BOOK 2
ANALYZING VULNERABILITIES: TECHNIQUES AND TOOLS FOR CYSA+ EXAM CS0-003

BOOK 3
THREAT INTELLIGENCE FUNDAMENTALS: ADVANCED STRATEGIES FOR CYSA+ EXAM CS0-003

BOOK 4
MASTERING INCIDENT RESPONSE: EXPERT TACTICS FOR CYSA+ EXAM CS0-003

ROB BOTWRIGHT

Published by Rob Botwright
Library of Congress Cataloging-in-Publication Data
ISBN 978-1-83938-794-4
Cover design by Rizzo

Disclaimer

The contents of this book are based on extensive research and the best available historical sources. However, the author and publisher make no claims, promises, or guarantees about the accuracy, completeness, or adequacy of the information contained herein. The information in this book is provided on an "as is" basis, and the author and publisher disclaim any and all liability for any errors, omissions, or inaccuracies in the information or for any actions taken in reliance on such information. The opinions and views expressed in this book are those of the author and do not necessarily reflect the official policy or position of any organization or individual mentioned in this book. Any reference to specific people, places, or events is intended only to provide historical context and is not intended to defame or malign any group, individual, or entity. The information in this book is intended for educational and entertainment purposes only. It is not intended to be a substitute for professional advice or judgment. Readers are encouraged to conduct their own research and to seek professional advice where appropriate. Every effort has been made to obtain necessary permissions and acknowledgments for all images and other copyrighted material used in this book. Any errors or omissions in this regard are unintentional, and the author and publisher will correct them in future editions.

BOOK 1 - FOUNDATIONS OF CYBERSECURITY: A BEGINNER'S GUIDE TO CYSA+ EXAM CS0-003

BOOK 2 - ANALYZING VULNERABILITIES: TECHNIQUES AND TOOLS FOR CYSA+ EXAM CS0-003

BOOK 3 - THREAT INTELLIGENCE FUNDAMENTALS: ADVANCED STRATEGIES FOR CYSA+ EXAM CS0-003

BOOK 4 - MASTERING INCIDENT RESPONSE: EXPERT TACTICS FOR CYSA+ EXAM CS0-003

Introduction

Welcome to the "CySA+ Study Guide: Exam CS0-003" bundle, an essential resource for aspiring cybersecurity professionals seeking to obtain the CompTIA Cybersecurity Analyst (CySA+) certification. This comprehensive bundle is designed to equip you with the knowledge, skills, and strategies needed to excel in the dynamic field of IT security.

Book 1, "Foundations of Cybersecurity: A Beginner's Guide to CySA+ Exam CS0-003," serves as your starting point on the journey to becoming a CySA+ certified professional. In this book, you will explore the fundamental concepts of cybersecurity, including network security, cryptography, and access control. Whether you're new to the field or looking to solidify your understanding of core principles, this book provides a solid foundation to build upon.

Book 2, "Analyzing Vulnerabilities: Techniques and Tools for CySA+ Exam CS0-003," delves into the critical area of vulnerability analysis. Here, you will learn various assessment techniques and tools used to identify and mitigate security weaknesses in systems and networks. From vulnerability scanning to penetration testing, this book equips you with the skills needed to assess and address vulnerabilities effectively.

Book 3, "Threat Intelligence Fundamentals: Advanced Strategies for CySA+ Exam CS0-003," explores the realm of threat intelligence, an increasingly crucial aspect of cybersecurity operations. In this book, you will discover advanced strategies for gathering, analyzing, and leveraging threat intelligence to enhance security posture. By understanding the tactics and motivations of adversaries, you will learn how to proactively identify and respond to emerging threats.

Book 4, "Mastering Incident Response: Expert Tactics for CySA+ Exam CS0-003," focuses on incident response, a critical component of cybersecurity defense. Here, you will gain valuable insights into developing incident response plans, conducting post-incident analysis, and implementing effective response strategies to mitigate the impact of security incidents. From containment to recovery, this book covers the entire incident response lifecycle.

Together, these four books form a comprehensive study guide for the CySA+ certification exam, covering all domains and objectives outlined in the exam syllabus. Whether you're looking to launch your career in cybersecurity or advance your existing skillset, this bundle provides the essential knowledge and practical guidance needed to succeed in today's cybersecurity landscape. Let's embark on this journey together and prepare to become certified CySA+ professionals!

BOOK 1
FOUNDATIONS OF CYBERSECURITY
A BEGINNER'S GUIDE TO CYSA+ EXAM CS0-003

ROB BOTWRIGHT

Chapter 1: Introduction to Cybersecurity Fundamentals

The evolution of cybersecurity has been a dynamic and continuous process, shaped by the ever-changing landscape of technology and the relentless ingenuity of cyber threats. It traces its origins back to the early days of computing when security concerns were relatively simple compared to the complex challenges faced today. In those nascent stages, cybersecurity primarily focused on physical security measures such as locked doors and guarded server rooms to protect mainframe computers from unauthorized access. However, with the rapid expansion of computer networks and the advent of the internet in the late 20th century, cybersecurity took on a new level of significance. As organizations began to connect their systems to the internet, they inadvertently exposed themselves to a myriad of vulnerabilities and threats. This paradigm shift necessitated the development of more sophisticated security measures to safeguard digital assets and sensitive information. Thus, the field of cybersecurity began to mature, evolving from basic perimeter defenses to more robust and comprehensive strategies. One of the pivotal milestones in this evolution was the emergence of encryption as a fundamental tool for securing data in transit and at rest. Encryption algorithms such as RSA and AES became integral components of cybersecurity protocols, enabling organizations to protect their communications and sensitive information from prying eyes. Moreover, the rise of cybercriminals and malicious actors further propelled the evolution of cybersecurity, as they continuously sought out new vulnerabilities to exploit for financial gain or malicious intent. Consequently, cybersecurity professionals were forced to adapt and innovate in response to these evolving threats, developing advanced techniques and technologies to detect, prevent, and mitigate cyber attacks. One such technique that revolutionized cybersecurity is the use of Intrusion Detection Systems (IDS) and Intrusion Prevention Systems (IPS), which monitor network traffic for suspicious activity and automatically block or alert administrators to potential threats. Deploying IDS/IPS involves configuring network devices to analyze traffic patterns and detect anomalous behavior, thereby strengthening the organization's defenses against cyber threats. Additionally, the advent of cloud computing and mobile technologies introduced new complexities to the cybersecurity landscape, as organizations grappled with securing distributed environments and diverse endpoints. This necessitated the development of specialized security solutions tailored to the unique challenges posed by cloud-based infrastructure and mobile devices. For example, Mobile Device Management (MDM) platforms enable organizations to enforce security policies and remotely manage mobile devices to prevent unauthorized access or data breaches. Similarly, cloud security platforms offer a range of services such as data encryption, identity and access management, and threat intelligence to protect sensitive data and workloads hosted in the cloud. Furthermore, the proliferation of Internet of Things (IoT) devices has expanded the attack surface, presenting new security risks and challenges for organizations across various industries. IoT devices, ranging from smart thermostats to industrial control systems, often lack built-in security features, making them vulnerable to exploitation by malicious actors.

To address these concerns, cybersecurity professionals have developed IoT security frameworks and best practices to mitigate risks associated with insecure IoT deployments. These frameworks encompass strategies such as device authentication, data encryption, and regular software updates to ensure the integrity and security of IoT ecosystems. Moreover, the convergence of cybersecurity with artificial intelligence and machine learning has opened up new possibilities for proactive threat detection and response. AI-powered security solutions leverage advanced algorithms to analyze vast amounts of data and identify patterns indicative of potential cyber threats. By automating threat detection and response processes, AI enhances the efficiency and effectiveness of cybersecurity operations, enabling organizations to stay one step ahead of cyber adversaries. In summary, the evolution of cybersecurity is an ongoing journey marked by innovation, adaptation, and resilience in the face of evolving threats. From its humble beginnings securing mainframe computers to its current state defending against sophisticated cyber attacks, cybersecurity has become an indispensable aspect of modern society. As technology continues to advance and cyber threats evolve, cybersecurity professionals must remain vigilant and proactive in their efforts to protect digital assets and safeguard the integrity of the digital ecosystem. Key concepts in cybersecurity encompass a broad array of principles and practices aimed at protecting digital assets and mitigating cyber threats in today's interconnected world. One fundamental concept is confidentiality, which refers to the assurance that sensitive information is accessible only to authorized individuals or entities. Achieving confidentiality involves implementing robust access control mechanisms, such as role-based access control (RBAC) or discretionary access control (DAC), to restrict unauthorized access to data. In addition to confidentiality, integrity is another critical concept in cybersecurity, ensuring that data remains accurate, consistent, and unaltered throughout its lifecycle. Maintaining data integrity involves implementing cryptographic techniques such as hashing or digital signatures to detect unauthorized modifications or tampering attempts. Moreover, availability is a key consideration in cybersecurity, ensuring that information and resources are accessible to authorized users when needed. Denial-of-Service (DoS) attacks, for example, aim to disrupt availability by overwhelming systems with a flood of malicious traffic, rendering them inaccessible to legitimate users. To mitigate the impact of DoS attacks, organizations can deploy intrusion prevention systems (IPS) or rate-limiting measures to filter and manage incoming traffic effectively. Another essential concept in cybersecurity is authentication, which verifies the identity of users or entities attempting to access systems or data. Common authentication mechanisms include passwords, biometric authentication, and multi-factor authentication (MFA), which combine two or more authentication factors for enhanced security. Deploying MFA typically involves configuring authentication servers or services such as Active Directory or OAuth to enforce additional verification steps, such as one-time passwords or biometric scans. Authorization is closely related to authentication, determining the actions or resources that authenticated users are permitted to access. Role-based access control (RBAC) is a prevalent authorization model that assigns permissions to users based on their roles or responsibilities within an organization. Administrators can manage RBAC policies using command-line interface (CLI) tools such as PowerShell or Linux shell commands to assign, modify, or revoke user permissions as needed. Accountability is another critical concept in cybersecurity, holding individuals or entities responsible for their actions and ensuring traceability in the event of security incidents or breaches. Implementing accountability mechanisms involves logging and auditing user activities, network traffic, and system events to maintain an accurate record of security-related events. Security Information and Event Management (SIEM) platforms facilitate centralized log management and analysis, allowing organizations to detect and investigate security incidents more effectively. Moreover, non-repudiation ensures that individuals cannot deny their actions or transactions, providing assurance that messages or transactions cannot be falsely denied by their originators. Digital signatures and cryptographic techniques play a vital role in achieving non-repudiation, providing evidence of the authenticity and integrity of electronic communications or transactions. Additionally, defense-in-depth is a fundamental cybersecurity strategy that employs multiple layers of security controls to protect against a diverse range of threats. Command-line tools such as iptables or Windows Firewall can be used to configure network firewalls and packet filtering rules, while intrusion detection systems (IDS) or intrusion prevention systems (IPS) monitor and block suspicious network traffic. Furthermore, endpoint security solutions such as antivirus software or host-based intrusion detection systems (HIDS) protect individual devices from malware infections or unauthorized access attempts. Patch management is another essential aspect of defense-in-depth, ensuring that systems and software are regularly updated with the latest security patches to address known vulnerabilities and mitigate the risk of exploitation. Moreover, security awareness and training are critical components of a robust cybersecurity posture, empowering users to recognize and respond to security threats effectively. Organizations can deploy phishing simulation tools or conduct security awareness training sessions to educate employees about common cyber threats and best practices for safeguarding sensitive information. Additionally, incident response planning and preparedness are essential for effectively responding to security incidents and minimizing their impact on organizational operations. Command-line tools such as Incident Response and Forensics Toolkit (IRFTK) or Volatility can be used to collect and analyze forensic evidence from compromised systems, aiding in the investigation and remediation of security incidents. By integrating these key concepts and practices into their cybersecurity strategies, organizations can enhance their resilience against cyber threats and safeguard their digital assets and operations.

Chapter 2: Understanding Threats and Vulnerabilities

Common types of cyber threats pose significant risks to individuals, organizations, and society at large, encompassing a diverse range of malicious activities perpetrated by cybercriminals and threat actors seeking financial gain, political motives, or disruption. One prevalent type of cyber threat is malware, malicious software designed to infiltrate and compromise computer systems, steal sensitive information, or disrupt normal operations. Deploying effective antivirus software such as Windows Defender or McAfee, organizations can detect and remove malware infections, safeguarding against potential data breaches or system disruptions. Another common cyber threat is phishing, a deceptive tactic used by cybercriminals to trick individuals into divulging sensitive information such as passwords, credit card numbers, or personal data. Implementing email filtering solutions such as Microsoft Exchange Online Protection (EOP) or Cisco Email Security, organizations can detect and block phishing emails before they reach users' inboxes, reducing the risk of data loss or identity theft. Moreover, ransomware represents a significant cyber threat, encrypting victims' files or systems and demanding payment for their decryption. Backup and recovery solutions such as Windows Server Backup or Veeam Backup & Replication enable organizations to restore encrypted files or systems from backup copies, mitigating the impact of ransomware attacks and minimizing data loss. Additionally, distributed denial-of-service (DDoS) attacks pose a severe threat to online services and websites, overwhelming servers with a flood of malicious traffic and rendering them inaccessible to legitimate users. Configuring network firewalls and intrusion prevention systems (IPS) using command-line interface (CLI) tools such as iptables or Cisco IOS, organizations can filter and block malicious traffic associated with DDoS attacks, maintaining the availability of their online services. Furthermore, insider threats represent a significant concern for organizations, as malicious or negligent insiders may exploit their access privileges to steal sensitive data, sabotage systems, or compromise network security. Implementing user access controls and monitoring solutions such as Microsoft Azure

Active Directory or SolarWinds Security Event Manager, organizations can detect and mitigate insider threats by monitoring user activities and enforcing least privilege principles. Moreover, supply chain attacks have become increasingly prevalent, targeting third-party vendors or service providers to gain unauthorized access to organizations' networks or systems. Conducting thorough vendor risk assessments and implementing supply chain security measures such as network segmentation or software supply chain integrity verification, organizations can mitigate the risk of supply chain attacks and protect their digital supply chains. Additionally, social engineering attacks exploit human psychology and trust to manipulate individuals into divulging sensitive information or performing actions that compromise security. Providing security awareness training and conducting simulated phishing exercises using tools such as KnowBe4 or PhishMe, organizations can educate employees about common social engineering tactics and empower them to recognize and report suspicious activities. Furthermore, zero-day exploits represent a significant cyber threat, exploiting previously unknown vulnerabilities in software or hardware to compromise systems or steal sensitive data. Deploying vulnerability management solutions such as Tenable.io or Qualys Vulnerability Management, organizations can identify and remediate zero-day vulnerabilities before they can be exploited by threat actors, reducing the risk of security breaches or data breaches. Additionally, advanced persistent threats (APTs) represent a sophisticated and stealthy cyber threat, targeting high-value assets or organizations over an extended period to steal sensitive information or conduct espionage. Implementing advanced threat detection and response solutions such as CrowdStrike Falcon or Palo Alto Networks Cortex XDR, organizations can detect and neutralize APTs by correlating and analyzing security events across their network environments. By understanding and mitigating these common types of cyber threats, organizations can enhance their cybersecurity posture and protect against potential data breaches, financial losses, or reputational damage. Vulnerability assessment techniques play a crucial role in identifying and mitigating security vulnerabilities within an organization's IT infrastructure, applications, and systems, ensuring the integrity, confidentiality, and availability of sensitive information and resources. One fundamental vulnerability assessment technique is network scanning, which involves scanning network devices and systems to identify potential vulnerabilities, misconfigurations, or security weaknesses. Command-line tools such as Nmap or OpenVAS can be used to perform comprehensive network scans, identifying open ports, services, and potential entry points for attackers. Additionally, vulnerability scanning tools such as Nessus or Qualys Vulnerability Management automate the process of identifying and prioritizing vulnerabilities across an organization's network infrastructure, enabling administrators to remediate them effectively. Another vulnerability assessment technique is web application scanning, which involves scanning web applications and websites for common security vulnerabilities such as SQL injection, cross-site scripting (XSS), or insecure authentication mechanisms. Deploying web application scanning tools such as OWASP ZAP or Burp Suite, organizations can identify and remediate vulnerabilities in their web applications, reducing the risk of data breaches or unauthorized access. Furthermore, endpoint scanning is a critical vulnerability assessment technique that involves scanning endpoint devices such as computers, laptops, or mobile devices for security vulnerabilities or compliance violations. Endpoint scanning solutions such as Microsoft Defender ATP or Symantec Endpoint Protection automate the process of scanning and remediation, enabling organizations to protect their endpoints from malware infections, data breaches, or unauthorized access attempts. Additionally, configuration auditing is an essential vulnerability assessment technique that involves auditing system configurations and settings to ensure compliance with security policies, industry standards, or regulatory requirements. Command-line tools such as PowerShell or Linux shell commands can be used to audit system configurations and settings, identifying deviations from baseline configurations or security best practices. Moreover, penetration testing is a proactive vulnerability assessment technique that involves simulating cyber attacks to identify and exploit security vulnerabilities in an organization's IT infrastructure, applications, or systems. Conducting penetration tests using tools such as Metasploit or Core Impact enables organizations to identify and remediate critical security vulnerabilities before they can be exploited by malicious actors. Furthermore, vulnerability management is a comprehensive approach to vulnerability assessment that involves identifying, prioritizing, and remedying security vulnerabilities across an organization's IT infrastructure, applications, and systems. Implementing vulnerability management solutions such as Rapid7 InsightVM or Tenable.io enables organizations to automate the process of vulnerability assessment, prioritization, and remediation, reducing the risk of security breaches or data breaches. Additionally, threat modeling is a proactive vulnerability assessment technique that involves identifying potential threats, vulnerabilities, and attack vectors in an organization's IT infrastructure, applications, or systems. Conducting threat modeling workshops or exercises enables organizations to identify and mitigate security risks before they can be exploited by malicious actors. Moreover, continuous monitoring is a fundamental vulnerability assessment technique that involves monitoring network traffic, system logs, and security events for indicators of compromise

(IOCs) or suspicious activities. Deploying security information and event management (SIEM) solutions such as Splunk or IBM QRadar enables organizations to detect and respond to security incidents in real-time, reducing the impact of cyber attacks or data breaches. By leveraging these vulnerability assessment techniques, organizations can enhance their cybersecurity posture and mitigate the risk of security breaches, data breaches, or unauthorized access to sensitive information and resources.

Chapter 3: Basics of Network Security

Network architecture and protocols form the foundation of modern communication systems, enabling the exchange of data and information between devices, systems, and users across diverse networks and environments, understanding network architecture involves examining the structure, components, and design principles that govern the operation of a network, the OSI (Open Systems Interconnection) model is a conceptual framework that defines the seven layers of communication within a network, from the physical layer, which deals with the transmission of raw data over physical media such as cables or wireless signals, to the application layer, which facilitates communication between software applications, each layer of the OSI model performs specific functions and interacts with adjacent layers to ensure the reliable transmission of data, TCP/IP (Transmission Control Protocol/Internet Protocol) is another widely used network protocol suite that defines the standards and rules for transmitting data over the internet and other networks, the TCP/IP model consists of four layers: the network interface layer, the internet layer, the transport layer, and the application layer, TCP/IP is the foundation of the internet and is used for communication between devices connected to the internet, including computers, servers, routers, and other network devices, understanding network protocols is essential for designing, implementing, and troubleshooting network architectures, protocols such as TCP (Transmission Control Protocol) and UDP (User Datagram Protocol) govern how data is transmitted between devices, while protocols such as IP (Internet Protocol) and ARP (Address Resolution Protocol) facilitate the routing and addressing of data packets within a network, configuring network devices and protocols often involves using command-line interface (CLI) tools such as Cisco IOS (Internetwork Operating System) or Linux shell commands, for example, configuring IP addresses on network interfaces in a Cisco router can be done using the following CLI commands: `interface FastEthernet0/0` (enters interface configuration mode), `ip address 192.168.1.1 255.255.255.0` (assigns an IP address and subnet mask to the interface), `no shutdown` (enables the interface), these commands configure the FastEthernet0/0 interface on the router with the IP address 192.168.1.1 and the subnet mask 255.255.255.0, network architecture design involves selecting the appropriate network topology, hardware components, and protocols to meet the requirements of an organization's communication needs, common network topologies include bus, star, ring, mesh, and hybrid topologies, each topology has its advantages and disadvantages in terms of scalability, fault tolerance, and cost, for example, a bus topology is simple and inexpensive to deploy but can suffer from performance degradation and single point of failure issues, while a mesh topology provides redundancy and fault tolerance but can be complex and expensive to implement, selecting the right network architecture and protocols requires careful consideration of factors such as network bandwidth, latency, reliability, security, and scalability, organizations must also consider the compatibility of network components and protocols with existing infrastructure and systems, ensuring seamless integration and interoperability, deploying network architecture and protocols involves configuring network devices such as routers, switches, firewalls, and access points to support communication between devices and networks, network administrators use CLI commands or graphical user interface (GUI) tools such as Cisco Packet Tracer or Wireshark to configure and monitor network devices and traffic, for example, configuring VLANs (Virtual Local Area Networks) on a Cisco switch can be done using the following CLI commands: `vlan 10` (creates VLAN 10), `name Sales` (assigns a name to the VLAN), `interface FastEthernet0/1` (enters interface configuration mode), `switchport mode access` (sets the interface to access mode), `switchport access vlan 10` (assigns the interface to VLAN 10), these commands create a VLAN named Sales and assign the FastEthernet0/1 interface to VLAN 10, ensuring that devices connected to that interface belong to the Sales VLAN, troubleshooting network architecture and protocols involves identifying and resolving issues related to connectivity, performance, and security, network administrators use diagnostic tools such as ping, traceroute, and netstat to troubleshoot network connectivity issues, while network monitoring tools such as Nagios or SolarWinds provide real-time visibility into network performance and security events, ensuring the reliability, availability, and security of network architecture and protocols is essential for organizations to maintain productivity, protect sensitive information, and mitigate the risk of cyber threats and attacks, implementing best practices such as regular network audits, security patches, and employee training can help organizations ensure the integrity and resilience of their network infrastructure. Firewall and Intrusion Detection Systems (IDS) are vital components of a comprehensive cybersecurity strategy, serving as the first line of defense against cyber threats and attacks, a firewall is a network security device that monitors and controls incoming and outgoing network traffic based on predetermined security rules or policies, there are several types of firewalls, including packet filtering firewalls, stateful inspection firewalls, and application layer firewalls, packet filtering firewalls inspect individual packets of data as they pass through the firewall and make filtering decisions based on criteria such as source IP address, destination IP address, port number, and protocol type, configuring packet filtering rules on a firewall often involves using CLI commands or GUI tools provided by the firewall vendor, for example, configuring an access control list (ACL) on a Cisco ASA firewall to allow inbound SSH (Secure Shell) traffic from a specific IP address range can be done using the following CLI commands: `access-list acl_name permit tcp source_ip source_mask destination_ip destination_mask eq ssh`, `access-group acl_name in interface interface_name`, these commands create an ACL named acl_name that permits TCP traffic from the specified source IP address range to the destination IP address on port 22 (SSH), and apply the ACL to the specified interface, stateful inspection firewalls maintain a stateful connection table to track the state of active network connections and make filtering decisions based on the context of the traffic, such as whether it is part of an established session or a new connection attempt, configuring stateful inspection rules on a firewall involves defining inspection policies for specific protocols or applications, and specifying the actions to take for different types of traffic, application layer firewalls operate at the application layer of the OSI model and inspect the content of network traffic to identify and block malicious or unauthorized activity, for example, a web application firewall (WAF) can inspect HTTP traffic to detect and block SQL injection attacks or cross-site scripting (XSS) attacks, deploying an application layer firewall often involves installing and configuring dedicated firewall appliances or software solutions that provide advanced inspection capabilities, intrusion detection systems (IDS) are network security devices or software applications that monitor network traffic for signs of suspicious or malicious activity, IDS can be classified into two main types: network-based intrusion detection systems (NIDS) and host-based intrusion detection systems (HIDS), network-based intrusion detection systems (NIDS) analyze network traffic in real-time to detect potential security threats or attacks, deploying a NIDS involves installing sensors or probes on network segments or devices to capture and analyze network traffic, for example, deploying Snort IDS on a Linux server involves installing the Snort software package using a package manager such as apt or yum, configuring the Snort ruleset to define the types of traffic to monitor and the actions to take when suspicious activity is detected, and starting the Snort service to begin monitoring network traffic, host-based intrusion detection systems (HIDS) monitor the activity and configuration of individual host systems to detect signs of compromise or unauthorized access, deploying a HIDS involves installing agent software on each host system to monitor system logs, file integrity, and user activity, for example, deploying OSSEC HIDS involves installing the OSSEC agent software on each host system using a package manager or manual installation, configuring the OSSEC agent to monitor system logs, file integrity, and user activity, and configuring the OSSEC server to receive and analyze alerts generated by the agent software, IDS generate alerts or notifications when suspicious activity is detected, such as attempts to exploit known vulnerabilities, unusual network traffic patterns, or unauthorized access attempts, analyzing and responding to IDS alerts involves investigating the source and nature of the activity, and taking appropriate action to mitigate the risk, such as blocking malicious IP addresses, quarantining infected systems, or updating firewall rules to prevent future attacks, integrating firewall and IDS technologies into a cohesive cybersecurity strategy enables organizations to detect, prevent, and respond to a wide range of cyber threats and attacks, ensuring the integrity, availability, and confidentiality of their data and resources.

Chapter 4: Principles of Access Control and Identity Management

Authentication methods and best practices are fundamental aspects of cybersecurity, ensuring that only authorized users gain access to systems, applications, and data, authentication is the process of verifying the identity of an individual or entity attempting to access resources, typically, authentication involves presenting credentials such as usernames and passwords, biometric data, or cryptographic tokens, one common authentication method is password-based authentication, which relies on users providing a secret password or passphrase to prove their identity, configuring password policies on systems and applications is essential to enforce strong password requirements and mitigate the risk of password-based attacks, for example, in a Linux environment, administrators can configure password policies using the `passwd` command to set parameters such as minimum password length, complexity requirements, and expiration intervals, another authentication method is multi-factor authentication (MFA), which requires users to provide two or more factors of authentication, such as something they know (e.g., a password), something they have (e.g., a security token), or something they are (e.g., a fingerprint), deploying MFA often involves configuring authentication servers or services such as Active Directory or Duo Security to enforce additional verification steps for user logins, such as sending one-time passcodes to mobile devices or requiring biometric scans, biometric authentication methods use unique physical characteristics such as fingerprints, facial features, or iris patterns to verify the identity of users, biometric authentication systems typically involve capturing biometric data using specialized hardware devices such as fingerprint scanners or facial recognition cameras, and comparing it against stored templates to authenticate users, deploying biometric authentication often involves integrating biometric hardware devices with authentication systems or applications, and configuring settings such as sensitivity thresholds and enrollment procedures, cryptographic authentication methods use digital certificates and cryptographic keys to verify the identity of users and secure communications, deploying cryptographic authentication involves generating and managing digital certificates using certificate authorities (CAs) or public key infrastructure (PKI) systems, and configuring systems and applications to use cryptographic protocols such as SSL/TLS for secure communication, token-based authentication methods use physical or virtual tokens to generate one-time passcodes or cryptographic keys for user authentication, deploying token-based authentication involves distributing physical tokens or installing token generator apps on users' devices, and configuring authentication servers or services to validate token-based authentication requests, best practices for authentication include implementing strong password policies, enforcing multi-factor authentication for sensitive systems and applications, regularly reviewing and updating authentication mechanisms and configurations, monitoring authentication logs for suspicious activity or unauthorized access attempts, educating users about security best practices and the importance of protecting their credentials, and integrating authentication technologies with other security controls such as firewalls, intrusion detection systems (IDS), and endpoint security solutions, by implementing robust authentication methods and following best practices, organizations can enhance the security of their systems, applications, and data, and reduce the risk of unauthorized access, data breaches, and identity theft. Role-Based Access Control (RBAC) is a widely used access control mechanism that restricts system access to authorized users based on their roles and responsibilities within an organization, RBAC simplifies access management by grouping users into roles and assigning permissions to those roles, rather than managing permissions individually for each user, implementing RBAC involves several key steps, including defining roles, assigning permissions, and mapping users to roles, the first step in RBAC implementation is to identify and define the roles within an organization, roles should be based on job functions, responsibilities, and access requirements, for example, an organization may have roles such as administrator, manager, employee, and guest, defining roles often involves conducting interviews with stakeholders and analyzing job descriptions and access requirements, once roles have been defined, the next step is to assign permissions to each role, permissions specify the actions or operations that users assigned to a role are allowed to perform, permissions can be defined at the system, application, or data level, depending on the granularity of access control required, for example, in a Linux environment, administrators can use the `chmod` command to set permissions on files and directories, specifying read, write, and execute permissions for different user roles, after assigning permissions to roles, the next step is to map users to roles, mapping involves associating individual users with the roles that correspond to their job functions and responsibilities, for example, in an Active Directory environment, administrators can use the `Add-ADGroupMember` PowerShell cmdlet to add users to security groups representing their roles, ensuring that users inherit the permissions assigned to those groups, RBAC implementation also involves enforcing segregation of duties (SoD) to prevent conflicts of interest and reduce the risk of fraud or abuse, SoD ensures that users are not assigned conflicting roles or permissions that could allow them to perform incompatible actions, for example, a user with the role of purchasing agent should not also have the role of accounts payable clerk, as this would create a conflict of interest, enforcing SoD often involves implementing access controls and auditing mechanisms to detect and remediate violations, RBAC can be implemented using built-in access control features provided by operating systems, applications, and databases, for example, in a Windows environment, administrators can use the Group Policy Management Console (GPMC) to create security groups representing different roles and assign permissions to those groups, ensuring that users inherit the appropriate access rights, RBAC can also be implemented using specialized identity and access management (IAM) solutions that provide centralized control and visibility over user access rights and permissions, IAM solutions often include features such as role provisioning, access certification, and policy enforcement, enabling organizations to implement RBAC across heterogeneous IT environments, RBAC implementation requires careful planning, coordination, and ongoing maintenance to ensure that access controls remain aligned with business requirements and security policies, organizations should regularly review and update role definitions, permissions, and user mappings to reflect changes in personnel, job roles, and access requirements, RBAC can help organizations improve security, streamline access management, and reduce the risk of data breaches and insider threats, by following best practices and leveraging automation tools, organizations can optimize RBAC implementation and achieve effective access control across their IT infrastructure.

Chapter 5: Introduction to Security Operations and Monitoring

Security Incident Management Process is a critical component of cybersecurity strategy, aiming to effectively detect, respond to, and recover from security incidents to minimize their impact on organizational operations and mitigate the risk of data breaches or unauthorized access, the incident management process typically involves several key phases, including preparation, detection, containment, eradication, recovery, and lessons learned, preparation involves establishing policies, procedures, and resources to support incident response activities, organizations should develop an incident response plan that outlines roles and responsibilities, communication protocols, escalation procedures, and technical tools and resources, for example, using the `Create-AzureRmSecurityPlan` PowerShell cmdlet, organizations can create a security plan in Microsoft Azure Security Center to define incident response roles and permissions, the incident detection phase involves monitoring and analyzing network traffic, system logs, and security alerts to identify signs of potential security incidents, organizations should deploy security monitoring tools such as intrusion detection systems (IDS), security information and event management (SIEM) systems, and endpoint detection and response (EDR) solutions to detect suspicious activity, for example, using the `Get-WinEvent` PowerShell cmdlet, administrators can query Windows event logs to search for indicators of compromise (IoCs) or anomalous behavior, containment is the process of isolating and limiting the scope of a security incident to prevent further damage or unauthorized access, containment measures may include disabling compromised user accounts, blocking malicious IP addresses, or segmenting network traffic, organizations should use network access control (NAC) policies, firewall rules, and endpoint security controls to contain incidents, for example, using the `netsh` command in Windows, administrators can configure firewall rules to block incoming and outgoing traffic to and from specific IP addresses, eradication involves identifying and removing the root cause of a security incident to prevent recurrence, organizations should conduct forensic analysis, malware analysis, and system audits to identify and remediate vulnerabilities or security weaknesses, for example, using the `Get-Process` PowerShell cmdlet, administrators can identify suspicious processes running on Windows systems and terminate them, the recovery phase involves restoring affected systems, applications, and data to normal operation and ensuring business continuity, organizations should use backup and recovery solutions to restore data from backup copies, apply security patches and updates, and implement additional security controls to prevent similar incidents in the future, for example, using the `Restore-AzRecoveryServicesBackupItem` PowerShell cmdlet, administrators can restore files and folders from Azure Backup to recover from data loss or corruption, the lessons learned phase involves conducting post-incident reviews and analysis to identify gaps in incident response procedures, training, or technology, organizations should document lessons learned, update incident response plans, and implement corrective actions to improve incident response capabilities, for example, using the `Invoke-WebRequest` PowerShell cmdlet, administrators can automate the collection of incident data and generate reports for analysis and review, continuous improvement is essential for effective security incident management, organizations should regularly review and update incident response plans, conduct tabletop exercises and simulations to test response procedures, and collaborate with industry peers and security experts to share best practices and lessons learned, for example, participating in information sharing and analysis centers (ISACs) or joining threat intelligence sharing communities can provide valuable insights into emerging threats and effective mitigation strategies, by following a structured incident management process and leveraging appropriate tools and resources, organizations can effectively detect, respond to, and recover from security incidents, minimizing the impact on operations and reducing the risk of data breaches or unauthorized access. Log management and analysis are essential components of cybersecurity operations, providing organizations with valuable insights into system activities, security events, and potential threats, log management involves collecting, storing, and analyzing logs generated by various IT systems, applications, and network devices, logs contain a wealth of information about user activities, system events, network traffic, and security incidents, including authentication attempts, file accesses, configuration changes, and security alerts, organizations should deploy log management solutions such as syslog servers, log management platforms, or security information and event management (SIEM) systems to centralize log collection and storage, for example, using the `syslog-ng` command in Linux, administrators can configure a syslog server to collect logs from multiple sources and store them in a centralized repository, log analysis involves parsing, correlating, and analyzing log data to identify patterns, anomalies, and security incidents, organizations should use log analysis tools and techniques such as log parsing, keyword searching, regular expressions, and statistical analysis to extract actionable insights from log data, for example, using the `grep` command in Linux, administrators can search log files for specific keywords or patterns, log management and analysis play a crucial role in cybersecurity operations, enabling organizations to detect and respond to security incidents, compliance violations, and operational issues, organizations should establish log management policies and procedures to govern the collection, retention, and analysis of log data, for example, defining retention periods, access controls, and audit trails for log data, log management and analysis can help organizations achieve compliance with regulatory requirements such as the Payment Card Industry Data Security Standard (PCI DSS), Health Insurance Portability and Accountability Act (HIPAA), and General Data Protection

Regulation (GDPR), organizations should integrate log management and analysis into their incident response processes to enhance visibility into security incidents and improve incident detection and response capabilities, for example, correlating log data with threat intelligence feeds can help identify indicators of compromise (IoCs) and prioritize incident response efforts, log management and analysis can also help organizations improve operational efficiency and optimize resource allocation by identifying performance bottlenecks, troubleshooting issues, and optimizing system configurations, for example, analyzing web server logs can help identify slow or failed requests, unauthorized access attempts, and potential denial-of-service (DoS) attacks, log management and analysis require careful planning, implementation, and ongoing maintenance to ensure effectiveness and reliability, organizations should define log management requirements, select appropriate log management tools and technologies, and establish processes for log collection, storage, analysis, and reporting, for example, configuring log rotation policies and archival processes to manage log storage requirements, log management and analysis should be integrated with other cybersecurity controls such as intrusion detection systems (IDS), antivirus solutions, and security information and event management (SIEM) systems to provide comprehensive visibility and threat detection capabilities, for example, aggregating logs from multiple sources into a centralized SIEM system can provide a unified view of security events and streamline incident response workflows, log management and analysis can also be enhanced with automation and machine learning techniques to improve scalability, accuracy, and efficiency, for example, using machine learning algorithms to analyze log data and identify anomalous behavior or security events, organizations should regularly review and update log management and analysis processes, tools, and procedures to adapt to evolving threats, technologies, and business requirements, for example, incorporating feedback from incident response exercises and security audits to refine log management and analysis practices, by implementing robust log management and analysis capabilities, organizations can improve their cybersecurity posture, enhance threat detection and response capabilities, and achieve greater visibility and control over their IT environments.

Chapter 6: Fundamentals of Incident Response and Recovery

Incident detection and classification are essential processes in cybersecurity operations, enabling organizations to identify and categorize security incidents promptly to initiate an effective response, incident detection involves monitoring network traffic, system logs, and security alerts to identify signs of potential security breaches or unauthorized access attempts, organizations should deploy detection tools and techniques such as intrusion detection systems (IDS), security information and event management (SIEM) systems, and endpoint detection and response (EDR) solutions to detect suspicious activity, for example, using the `Snort` command in Linux, administrators can deploy a network IDS to analyze network traffic and detect potential intrusions, incident classification involves categorizing security incidents based on their severity, impact, and type, organizations should establish incident classification criteria and procedures to ensure consistent and accurate classification of incidents, for example, defining incident severity levels such as critical, high, medium, and low, and specifying response procedures and escalation paths for each severity level, incident detection and classification play a crucial role in effective incident response, enabling organizations to prioritize and allocate resources based on the severity and impact of security incidents, organizations should establish incident response teams and procedures to facilitate timely detection, classification, and response to security incidents, for example, defining roles and responsibilities for incident responders, establishing communication channels and escalation procedures, and conducting regular training and exercises to ensure readiness, incident detection and classification should be integrated with other cybersecurity controls such as access controls, encryption, and monitoring to provide comprehensive protection against security threats, for example, correlating security alerts from IDS, SIEM, and EDR solutions to identify and prioritize incidents, incident detection and classification should also be aligned with regulatory requirements and industry best practices to ensure compliance and effectiveness, for example, complying with incident reporting and notification requirements specified in regulations such as the General Data Protection Regulation (GDPR) and the Health Insurance Portability and Accountability Act (HIPAA), incident detection and classification require continuous monitoring and analysis of security events and logs to identify anomalies and potential indicators of compromise (IoCs), organizations should use advanced analytics, machine learning, and threat intelligence to enhance detection capabilities and reduce false positives, for example, using anomaly detection algorithms to identify deviations from normal behavior and detect potential threats, incident detection and classification should be supported by robust incident response processes and procedures to ensure timely and effective response to security incidents, organizations should establish incident response playbooks and workflows to guide responders through the detection, classification, containment, eradication, and recovery phases of incident response, for example, defining response actions and decision criteria for each incident type and severity level, incident detection and classification should be continuously evaluated and refined based on lessons learned and feedback from incident response exercises and post-incident reviews, organizations should conduct regular assessments of detection and classification capabilities, identify gaps and areas for improvement, and implement corrective actions to enhance effectiveness, for example, conducting tabletop exercises to simulate different types of security incidents and evaluate response procedures, incident detection and classification are critical components of a proactive cybersecurity strategy, enabling organizations to detect and respond to security threats before they can cause significant damage or disruption, by implementing robust detection and classification processes, organizations can strengthen their security posture, mitigate the impact of security incidents, and protect sensitive data and assets from unauthorized access and exploitation. Incident containment and eradication techniques are crucial aspects of cybersecurity incident response, aimed at minimizing the impact of security incidents and restoring affected systems to a secure state, incident containment involves isolating and limiting the scope of a security incident to prevent further damage or unauthorized access, organizations should deploy containment measures such as network segmentation, access controls, and endpoint isolation to prevent the spread of malware and limit the attacker's ability to move laterally within the network, for example, using the `ipconfig` command in Windows, administrators can disable network interfaces or configure firewall rules to block communication between infected and unaffected systems, incident eradication involves identifying and removing the root cause of a security incident to prevent recurrence, organizations should conduct forensic analysis, malware analysis, and system audits to identify and remediate vulnerabilities or security weaknesses exploited by attackers, for example, using the `netstat` command in Linux, administrators can identify suspicious network connections or listening ports and terminate malicious processes, incident containment and eradication should be conducted promptly and methodically to minimize the duration and impact of security incidents, organizations should establish incident response teams and procedures to facilitate rapid containment and eradication of security incidents, for example, defining roles and responsibilities for incident responders, establishing communication channels and escalation procedures, and conducting regular training and exercises to ensure readiness, incident containment and eradication should be guided by incident response playbooks and workflows that outline step-by-step procedures and response actions, organizations should define response actions and decision criteria for different types of security incidents, specifying containment and eradication measures based on the severity and impact of the incident, for example, defining containment actions such as isolating affected systems from the network or disabling compromised user accounts, and specifying eradication actions such as removing malware, patching vulnerabilities, and restoring affected systems from backup, incident containment and eradication should be coordinated with other incident response activities such as detection, analysis, and recovery to ensure a cohesive and effective response, organizations should communicate with stakeholders, such as executive management, legal counsel, and regulatory authorities, to provide updates on containment and eradication efforts, and to coordinate response actions, incident containment and eradication should be followed by post-incident activities such as lessons learned and post-incident reviews to identify areas for improvement and implement corrective actions, organizations should conduct debriefings with incident responders to gather feedback and insights on the effectiveness of containment and eradication efforts, and to identify lessons learned and best practices for future incidents, incident containment and eradication techniques should be continuously evaluated and updated to adapt to evolving threats and technologies, organizations should conduct regular assessments of incident response capabilities, including containment and eradication techniques, to identify gaps and areas for improvement, and to ensure readiness for future security incidents, incident containment and eradication are critical components of effective incident response, enabling organizations to minimize the impact of security incidents and restore affected systems to a secure state, by implementing robust containment and eradication techniques, organizations can mitigate the risk of data breaches, financial losses, and reputational damage, and protect sensitive data and assets from unauthorized access and exploitation.

Chapter 7: Exploring Security Technologies and Tools

Antivirus and anti-malware solutions are essential components of cybersecurity defense strategies, designed to protect systems and networks from malicious software and cyber threats, antivirus software detects, blocks, and removes known and unknown malware, including viruses, worms, Trojans, ransomware, and spyware, organizations should deploy antivirus solutions on endpoints, servers, and network devices to provide comprehensive protection against malware, for example, using the `apt install clamav` command in Linux, administrators can install the ClamAV antivirus software to scan files and directories for malware, antivirus software uses signature-based detection, heuristic analysis, and behavior monitoring to identify and block malicious software, signature-based detection compares file signatures and patterns against a database of known malware signatures, heuristic analysis identifies suspicious behavior patterns and characteristics associated with malware, and behavior monitoring observes system activities and alerts on anomalous behavior indicative of malware infection, organizations should configure antivirus software to perform regular scans of files, directories, and system memory to detect and remove malware, for example, using the `clamscan` command in Linux, administrators can scan files and directories for malware using the ClamAV antivirus engine, antivirus software should be configured to automatically update virus definitions and software patches to ensure protection against the latest threats, organizations should deploy endpoint protection platforms (EPP) and next-generation antivirus (NGAV) solutions that offer advanced features such as endpoint detection and response (EDR), threat intelligence, and machine learning, for example, deploying CrowdStrike Falcon or Carbon Black CB Defense to provide real-time threat detection and response capabilities, anti-malware solutions complement antivirus software by providing additional layers of protection against malware, including zero-day exploits, fileless malware, and advanced persistent threats (APTs), organizations should deploy anti-malware solutions such as anti-exploit, anti-ransomware, and anti-rootkit tools to protect against specific types of malware attacks, for example, deploying Malwarebytes Anti-Exploit or HitmanPro.Alert to prevent exploit-based attacks, antivirus and anti-malware solutions should be integrated with other security controls such as firewalls, intrusion detection systems (IDS), and security information and event management (SIEM) systems to provide comprehensive threat detection and response capabilities, for example, integrating antivirus logs with SIEM platforms such as Splunk or ELK (Elasticsearch, Logstash, and Kibana) to correlate security events and generate actionable alerts, organizations should conduct regular security assessments and penetration tests to evaluate the effectiveness of antivirus and anti-malware solutions in detecting and mitigating threats, for example, using penetration testing tools such as Metasploit or Nmap to simulate real-world attacks and assess the resilience of security controls, antivirus and anti-malware solutions should be continuously monitored and updated to adapt to evolving threats and technologies, organizations should subscribe to threat intelligence feeds and security advisories to stay informed about emerging threats and vulnerabilities, and to proactively update security controls and policies, antivirus and anti-malware solutions play a critical role in protecting organizations against cyber threats, helping to prevent data breaches, financial losses, and reputational damage, by deploying robust antivirus and anti-malware solutions and integrating them with other security controls, organizations can enhance their cybersecurity posture and mitigate the risk of malware infections and cyber attacks. Security Information and Event Management (SIEM) tools are essential components of cybersecurity infrastructure, providing organizations with centralized visibility into security events and logs from across their IT environment, SIEM solutions aggregate and correlate data from various sources such as network devices, servers, applications, and security controls to detect and respond to security incidents, organizations should deploy SIEM solutions to collect, analyze, and manage security event data, for example, using the `yum install rsyslog-gnutls` command in Linux, administrators can install the Rsyslog package to collect and forward syslog data to a SIEM server, SIEM solutions collect data from different sources using protocols such as syslog, SNMP, WMI, and API integrations, organizations should configure log sources to send data to the SIEM server using standardized formats and protocols, for example, configuring network devices to forward syslog messages to the SIEM server using the `logging` command in Cisco IOS, SIEM solutions normalize and parse log data to extract relevant information such as timestamps, source IP addresses, event IDs, and user identities, organizations should configure parsing rules and filters to extract and categorize log data based on predefined criteria, for example, using regular expressions to extract IP addresses or user names from log messages, SIEM solutions correlate and analyze log data to identify patterns, trends, and anomalies indicative of security incidents, organizations should configure correlation rules and use cases to detect common attack patterns such as brute-force attacks, malware infections, and data exfiltration, for example, configuring correlation rules to trigger alerts when multiple failed login attempts are detected from the same IP address, SIEM solutions provide real-time monitoring and alerting capabilities to notify security teams of potential security incidents, organizations should configure alerting thresholds and notification policies to prioritize and escalate alerts based on their severity and impact, for example, configuring email or SMS alerts for critical security events, SIEM solutions enable organizations to investigate security incidents by providing interactive dashboards, search capabilities, and forensic analysis tools, organizations should conduct incident investigations using SIEM tools to identify the root cause of security incidents, analyze the impact, and implement remediation measures, for example, using the search query language (SQL) in

Splunk or Elasticsearch to search and analyze log data, SIEM solutions support compliance reporting and audit trail generation by providing predefined reports, dashboards, and templates for common regulatory requirements such as PCI DSS, HIPAA, and GDPR, organizations should configure compliance reports and dashboards to monitor and report on security controls and policy violations, for example, generating monthly reports on user account changes, access permissions, and security incidents, SIEM solutions integrate with other security controls such as firewalls, intrusion detection systems (IDS), and endpoint security solutions to provide comprehensive threat detection and response capabilities, organizations should integrate SIEM with security orchestration, automation, and response (SOAR) platforms to automate incident response workflows and streamline response processes, for example, integrating SIEM with the Phantom or Demisto SOAR platforms to orchestrate response actions such as isolating infected endpoints or blocking malicious IP addresses, SIEM solutions require ongoing tuning, optimization, and maintenance to ensure effectiveness and reliability, organizations should regularly review and update correlation rules, alerting thresholds, and data retention policies to adapt to evolving threats and technologies, for example, tuning correlation rules to reduce false positives or increasing log retention periods to comply with regulatory requirements, SIEM solutions play a crucial role in enhancing organizations' cybersecurity posture, enabling proactive threat detection, rapid incident response, and effective compliance management, by deploying robust SIEM solutions and integrating them with other security controls, organizations can strengthen their defenses, mitigate the risk of security breaches, and protect sensitive data and assets from cyber threats.

Chapter 8: Essentials of Cryptography

Cryptographic algorithms and techniques are fundamental tools in cybersecurity, enabling secure communication, data protection, and authentication in digital environments, cryptographic algorithms use mathematical functions to transform plaintext data into ciphertext, ensuring confidentiality and integrity of sensitive information, organizations should deploy cryptographic algorithms such as Advanced Encryption Standard (AES), Rivest-Shamir-Adleman (RSA), and Elliptic Curve Cryptography (ECC) to encrypt data at rest and in transit, for example, using the OpenSSL library to encrypt a file with AES encryption, cryptographic techniques such as symmetric and asymmetric encryption are used to protect data confidentiality, symmetric encryption uses a single key to encrypt and decrypt data, organizations should use symmetric encryption algorithms such as AES to secure data communication and storage, for example, using the `openssl enc` command to encrypt a file with AES encryption and the `openssl aes-256-cbc` command to specify the AES encryption algorithm and mode, asymmetric encryption uses a pair of public and private keys to encrypt and decrypt data, organizations should use asymmetric encryption algorithms such as RSA and ECC for key exchange, digital signatures, and secure communication, for example, using the `openssl genrsa` command to generate a RSA key pair and the `openssl rsa -in private.key -out public.pem -pubout` command to extract the public key from the RSA private key, cryptographic hashing algorithms are used to generate unique fixed-length hash values from input data, ensuring data integrity and authentication, organizations should deploy cryptographic hashing algorithms such as Secure Hash Algorithm (SHA) and Message Digest Algorithm (MD) to generate hash values for password storage, digital signatures, and data integrity verification, for example, using the `sha256sum` command to calculate the SHA-256 hash value of a file in Linux, cryptographic key management is essential for secure encryption and decryption, organizations should implement key management policies and procedures to generate, store, distribute, and revoke cryptographic keys securely, for example, using the `openssl rand` command to generate a random symmetric encryption key and the `openssl rsa -aes256 -in private.key -out encrypted.key` command to encrypt a symmetric encryption key with an RSA public key, cryptographic protocols such as Transport Layer Security (TLS) and Pretty Good Privacy (PGP) are used to secure network communication and email messaging, organizations should deploy cryptographic protocols to establish secure communication channels and protect sensitive data during transmission, for example, using the `openssl s_client` command to test TLS connectivity to a server and the `gpg --encrypt -- recipient user@example.com message.txt` command to encrypt an email message with PGP, cryptographic algorithms and techniques play a crucial role in protecting sensitive information and maintaining trust in digital transactions, organizations should select and deploy cryptographic algorithms and techniques based on their security requirements, performance considerations, and compliance obligations, for example, complying with regulatory requirements such as the Payment Card Industry Data Security Standard (PCI DSS) and the General Data Protection Regulation (GDPR) by using approved cryptographic algorithms and key management practices, cryptographic algorithms and techniques should be continuously evaluated and updated to address emerging threats and vulnerabilities, organizations should monitor cryptographic vulnerabilities and security advisories to identify and remediate weaknesses in cryptographic implementations, for example, patching systems to mitigate vulnerabilities such as the OpenSSL Heartbleed vulnerability, cryptographic algorithms and techniques should be integrated with other security controls such as access controls, encryption, and authentication mechanisms to provide layered defense against cyber threats, organizations should implement cryptographic best practices such as using strong encryption algorithms, protecting cryptographic keys, and regularly updating cryptographic libraries and protocols, for example, rotating encryption keys regularly to mitigate the risk of key compromise and using hardware security modules (HSMs) to protect cryptographic keys, by deploying robust cryptographic algorithms and techniques and adhering to cryptographic best practices, organizations can enhance their cybersecurity posture, protect sensitive data, and ensure the confidentiality, integrity, and authenticity of digital information. Public Key Infrastructure (PKI) concepts form the foundation of secure communication and authentication in modern digital environments, PKI is a framework of cryptographic techniques and protocols that enable secure exchange of digital certificates and encryption keys, organizations should deploy PKI to establish trust, confidentiality, and integrity in digital transactions and communications, for example, using the `openssl req` command to generate a Certificate Signing Request (CSR) for requesting a digital certificate from a Certificate Authority (CA), PKI relies on asymmetric encryption algorithms such as RSA and ECC to generate key pairs consisting of public and private keys, organizations should generate key pairs for digital signatures, encryption, and authentication purposes, for example, using the `openssl genrsa` command to generate a RSA key pair, PKI uses digital certificates to bind public keys to identities and verify the authenticity of digital signatures, organizations should issue digital certificates using a trusted CA to authenticate users, devices, and services, for example, using the `openssl x509` command to generate a self-signed digital certificate for a web server, PKI components include Certificate Authorities (CAs), Registration Authorities (RAs), Certificate Revocation Lists (CRLs), and Online Certificate Status Protocol (OCSP) responders, organizations should deploy PKI components to manage digital certificates and ensure their validity and integrity, for example, configuring a CA using Microsoft Active Directory Certificate Services or OpenSSL, PKI supports various certificate formats such as X.509, PGP, and

S/MIME for different use cases such as web server authentication, email encryption, and code signing, organizations should select appropriate certificate formats based on their security requirements and interoperability needs, for example, generating a X.509 certificate for a web server using the `openssl req` command, PKI provides mechanisms for certificate enrollment, renewal, and revocation to maintain the security and validity of digital certificates, organizations should implement certificate lifecycle management processes to manage certificate issuance, renewal, and revocation, for example, configuring certificate auto-enrollment and renewal policies using Microsoft Group Policy, PKI integrates with other security controls such as encryption, digital signatures, and authentication mechanisms to provide comprehensive security solutions, organizations should deploy PKI in conjunction with encryption technologies such as Secure Sockets Layer (SSL) and Transport Layer Security (TLS) to secure network communication, for example, configuring SSL/TLS certificates for web servers and endpoints, PKI enables secure authentication and access control through mechanisms such as smart cards, digital signatures, and multi-factor authentication, organizations should deploy PKI-based authentication solutions to verify the identity of users and devices, for example, configuring smart card authentication using Active Directory Certificate Services and smart card readers, PKI facilitates secure email communication and document exchange through encryption and digital signatures, organizations should deploy PKI-based email encryption and signing solutions to protect sensitive information and verify the integrity of digital documents, for example, configuring S/MIME encryption and signing for email clients such as Microsoft Outlook, PKI supports identity federation and single sign-on (SSO) for seamless access to multiple applications and services, organizations should deploy PKI-based identity federation solutions to enable secure access to cloud-based and on-premises resources, for example, configuring Security Assertion Markup Language (SAML) authentication for web applications, PKI enables secure code execution and software distribution through code signing certificates, organizations should sign software executables and scripts using PKI-based code signing certificates to verify their authenticity and integrity, for example, signing software packages using Microsoft Authenticode or Java code signing tools, PKI standards such as X.509, PKCS, and LDAP provide interoperable frameworks for implementing PKI solutions across different platforms and environments, organizations should adhere to PKI standards and best practices to ensure compatibility and interoperability of PKI components, for example, following X.509 certificate format specifications for digital certificate generation and management, PKI plays a critical role in enabling secure communication, authentication, and trust in digital transactions and interactions, organizations should deploy robust PKI solutions and adhere to PKI best practices to mitigate the risk of data breaches, fraud, and unauthorized access, for example, implementing PKI policies and procedures to govern certificate issuance, renewal, and revocation processes.

Chapter 9: Overview of Compliance and Legal Considerations

Regulatory compliance frameworks are essential guidelines and standards that organizations must adhere to in order to ensure the security, privacy, and integrity of their data and systems, compliance frameworks provide a structured approach to managing and mitigating risks associated with various regulatory requirements and industry standards, organizations operating in regulated industries such as finance, healthcare, and government are subject to compliance mandates aimed at protecting sensitive information and maintaining trust with stakeholders, for example, the Payment Card Industry Data Security Standard (PCI DSS) mandates specific security controls for organizations that handle credit card transactions, compliance frameworks such as the Health Insurance Portability and Accountability Act (HIPAA) and the General Data Protection Regulation (GDPR) impose requirements for protecting healthcare data and personal information, respectively, organizations should assess their compliance obligations based on their industry, geographic location, and business activities, for example, conducting a gap analysis to identify areas of non-compliance with regulatory requirements, compliance frameworks provide detailed requirements and controls for addressing specific security and privacy concerns, organizations should implement controls and measures to address compliance requirements such as data encryption, access controls, and audit logging, for example, encrypting sensitive data at rest and in transit using encryption algorithms such as AES and TLS, compliance frameworks require organizations to establish policies, procedures, and documentation to demonstrate compliance with regulatory requirements, organizations should develop and maintain policies such as acceptable use policies, data retention policies, and incident response plans to ensure compliance with regulatory mandates, for example, developing an incident response plan outlining procedures for responding to security incidents and data breaches, compliance frameworks mandate regular risk assessments and audits to evaluate the effectiveness of security controls and measures, organizations should conduct risk assessments and audits to identify vulnerabilities, assess risks, and verify compliance with regulatory requirements, for example, conducting vulnerability scans and penetration tests to identify security weaknesses, compliance frameworks require organizations to implement controls and measures to protect sensitive information and prevent unauthorized access, organizations should deploy security controls such as firewalls, intrusion detection systems (IDS), and data loss prevention (DLP) solutions to safeguard data and systems from cyber threats, for example, configuring firewall rules to restrict unauthorized access to network resources, compliance frameworks mandate data protection measures such as encryption, data masking, and access controls to protect sensitive information from unauthorized disclosure, organizations should implement encryption and access controls to protect sensitive data stored in databases, file systems, and cloud storage platforms, for example, using encryption algorithms such as AES to encrypt data before storing it in a database, compliance frameworks require organizations to implement security awareness training programs to educate employees about security risks and best practices, organizations should provide security awareness training to employees to raise awareness about security threats and promote good security hygiene, for example, conducting phishing simulations and security awareness workshops to educate employees about common phishing attacks and how to avoid them, compliance frameworks mandate incident response and breach notification requirements to ensure timely detection, response, and reporting of security incidents, organizations should establish incident response procedures and notification processes to respond to security incidents and data breaches, for example, developing incident response playbooks outlining procedures for detecting, containing, and mitigating security incidents, compliance frameworks provide guidelines and standards for achieving and maintaining compliance with regulatory requirements, organizations should regularly review and update their compliance programs to address changes in regulations, technology, and business operations, for example, conducting regular reviews of compliance policies and procedures to ensure alignment with regulatory requirements, compliance frameworks play a crucial role in promoting trust, transparency, and accountability in organizations' security and privacy practices, organizations should prioritize compliance efforts to protect sensitive information, maintain regulatory compliance, and uphold their reputation and trustworthiness with customers, partners, and stakeholders. Legal issues in cybersecurity encompass a wide range of concerns related to laws, regulations, and legal frameworks that govern the use, protection, and management of digital information and systems, organizations operating in the digital realm are subject to various legal obligations and liabilities aimed at safeguarding the confidentiality, integrity, and availability of data, for example, the European Union's General Data Protection Regulation (GDPR) imposes strict requirements for protecting personal data and imposes significant penalties for non-compliance, legal issues in cybersecurity include privacy laws, data protection regulations, intellectual property rights, and cybercrime statutes, organizations should understand and comply with relevant laws and regulations to avoid legal repercussions and mitigate risks, for example, implementing measures such as data encryption, access controls, and security awareness training to comply with data protection laws, privacy laws such as the California Consumer Privacy Act (CCPA) and the Health Insurance Portability and Accountability Act (HIPAA) regulate the collection, use, and disclosure of personal information, organizations should implement privacy policies and procedures to protect sensitive data and ensure compliance with privacy regulations, for example, developing a privacy policy that outlines how personal information is collected, used, and shared, data breach notification laws require organizations to notify affected individuals and regulatory authorities in the event of a security incident involving personal data, organizations should establish incident response plans and notification processes to comply with data breach notification requirements, for example, developing a data breach response plan that outlines procedures for detecting, containing, and reporting security incidents, intellectual property laws protect organizations' proprietary information, trade secrets, and creative works from unauthorized use, organizations should implement measures such as confidentiality agreements, copyright protection, and trademark registration to safeguard intellectual property rights, for example, implementing access controls and encryption to protect trade secrets and confidential information, cybercrime laws such as the Computer Fraud and Abuse Act (CFAA) and the Cybersecurity Information Sharing Act (CISA) prohibit unauthorized access to computer systems, data theft, and cyber attacks, organizations should implement security controls and incident response procedures to prevent, detect, and mitigate cybercrime, for example, deploying firewalls, intrusion detection systems (IDS), and security information and event management (SIEM) solutions to protect against cyber threats, regulatory compliance is a key aspect of legal issues in cybersecurity, organizations should assess their legal obligations based on their industry, geographic location, and business activities, for example, conducting a compliance gap analysis to identify areas of non-compliance with relevant laws and regulations, legal issues in cybersecurity extend to contractual agreements, liability issues, and jurisdictional considerations, organizations should review and negotiate contracts, service level agreements (SLAs), and terms of service to address legal and regulatory requirements related to cybersecurity, for example, including provisions for data protection, breach notification, and indemnification in vendor contracts, cybersecurity litigation and enforcement actions pose legal risks and liabilities for organizations, organizations should prepare for potential legal disputes and regulatory investigations by maintaining accurate records, documenting security measures, and engaging legal counsel, for example, retaining legal counsel to provide guidance on cybersecurity legal issues and represent the organization in legal proceedings, cybersecurity compliance audits and assessments help organizations evaluate their legal compliance posture and identify areas for improvement, organizations should conduct regular audits and assessments to assess their compliance with legal and regulatory requirements, for example, conducting an annual cybersecurity compliance audit to evaluate controls, policies, and procedures, legal issues in cybersecurity are dynamic and evolving, organizations should stay informed about changes in laws, regulations, and industry standards to ensure ongoing compliance and risk management, for example, monitoring legal developments and regulatory updates through industry associations, legal counsel, and government agencies.

Chapter 10: Preparing for the CySA+ Exam CS0-003

The Exam Overview and Objectives provide a comprehensive understanding of the examination structure, content, and goals, helping candidates prepare effectively for the certification exam, understanding the exam overview and objectives is crucial for planning study strategies, identifying areas of strength and weakness, and maximizing the chances of success, candidates should review the exam objectives thoroughly to ensure alignment with their knowledge and skills, for example, accessing the official exam objectives document provided by the certification body, the exam overview typically includes information about the exam format, duration, number of questions, and passing score requirements, candidates should familiarize themselves with the exam format to simulate test conditions and manage time effectively during the exam, for example, reviewing sample questions and taking practice tests to gauge readiness and build confidence, the exam objectives outline the knowledge domains, topics, and subtopics covered in the exam, candidates should assess their proficiency in each domain and prioritize study efforts accordingly, for example, using study guides, textbooks, and online resources to cover exam objectives systematically, the exam objectives are often organized into categories or domains representing different areas of expertise, candidates should review each domain to identify specific skills and knowledge areas required for the exam, for example, breaking down exam objectives into manageable study units and setting study goals for each domain, the exam objectives provide detailed descriptions of the knowledge, skills, and tasks expected of candidates, candidates should assess their readiness against each objective and seek additional resources or training if needed, for example, enrolling in training courses, workshops, or boot camps to fill knowledge gaps and reinforce skills, the exam objectives may include references to relevant textbooks, whitepapers, articles, and documentation, candidates should use these references to supplement their study materials and deepen their understanding of exam topics, for example, accessing recommended reading materials and studying additional resources for in-depth coverage of exam objectives, the exam objectives may also include practical skills and hands-on tasks that candidates need to demonstrate proficiency in, candidates should practice these skills in a lab environment or virtual sandbox to gain practical experience, for example, setting up virtual machines, configuring network devices, and performing security assessments to apply theoretical knowledge in real-world scenarios, the exam objectives serve as a roadmap for exam preparation and self-assessment, candidates should periodically review their progress against the exam objectives and adjust their study plan accordingly, for example, tracking study hours, completing practice exams, and monitoring performance metrics to measure progress, the exam objectives are periodically updated to reflect changes in technology, industry trends, and job roles, candidates should stay informed about updates to the exam objectives and incorporate new topics or skills into their study plan, for example, subscribing to certification newsletters, forums, or social media channels to receive updates and announcements, the exam objectives provide a framework for professional development and career advancement, achieving certification demonstrates competency and expertise in cybersecurity, candidates should leverage their certification to pursue career opportunities, promotions, and salary advancements, for example, updating resumes,

LinkedIn profiles, and professional networking profiles to showcase certification achievements, the exam objectives reflect industry standards, best practices, and emerging trends in cybersecurity, candidates should apply their knowledge and skills gained from exam preparation to address real-world challenges and contribute to organizational success, for example, implementing security controls, conducting risk assessments, and advising stakeholders on cybersecurity matters, the exam objectives play a vital role in maintaining the relevance and credibility of the certification, candidates should provide feedback and suggestions for improving the exam objectives to the certification body, for example, participating in surveys, focus groups, or advisory committees to share insights and experiences, the exam objectives serve as a guidepost for continuous learning and skill development, candidates should pursue ongoing education, training, and certifications to stay current with evolving technologies and industry practices, for example, attending conferences, webinars, and workshops to learn about new tools, techniques, and strategies in cybersecurity. Study tips and resources are essential for success in preparing for certification exams and advancing one's knowledge and skills in cybersecurity, candidates should establish a structured study plan to organize their study sessions, set goals, and track progress effectively, for example, creating a study schedule with specific objectives and milestones, consistency is key to successful exam preparation, candidates should allocate dedicated time each day or week for studying, reviewing materials, and practicing exam questions, for example, setting aside a few hours every evening or weekends for focused study sessions, candidates should identify their learning preferences and tailor their study approach accordingly, for example, using visual aids, hands-on labs, or audio recordings to reinforce learning, active learning techniques such as summarizing, teaching others, and solving problems can enhance understanding and retention of information, candidates should actively engage with study materials and practice exams to reinforce concepts and identify areas for improvement, for example, explaining concepts to a study partner, discussing topics in online forums, or participating in study groups, leveraging multiple learning resources such as textbooks, online courses, video tutorials, and practice exams can provide diverse perspectives and reinforce understanding, candidates should explore different study resources to find the ones that best suit their learning style and preferences, for example, using official study guides, training courses, and supplementary materials from reputable sources, practice exams are valuable tools for assessing readiness and familiarizing oneself with the exam format and question types, candidates should take practice exams under simulated test conditions to simulate the exam experience and identify areas of weakness, for example, using exam simulators or practice test platforms to gauge readiness and build confidence, reviewing exam objectives and focusing on areas of weakness can help prioritize study efforts and ensure comprehensive coverage of exam topics, candidates should regularly review exam objectives and assess their progress against each objective to stay on track with their study plan, for example, periodically reviewing exam objectives and adjusting study priorities based on progress, seeking support from peers, mentors, and study groups can provide motivation, encouragement, and valuable insights for exam preparation, candidates should engage with fellow learners, participate in online forums, and seek guidance from experienced professionals to overcome challenges and stay motivated, for example, joining online communities, forums, or study groups dedicated to cybersecurity certification exams, taking breaks, staying healthy, and managing stress are important for maintaining focus and productivity during exam preparation, candidates should prioritize self-care, exercise, and relaxation techniques to manage stress and avoid burnout, for example, practicing mindfulness, meditation, or deep breathing exercises, maintaining a positive mindset, setting realistic goals, and celebrating small victories can boost morale and keep candidates motivated throughout their exam preparation journey, candidates should stay organized, track progress, and adapt their study plan as needed to ensure effective and efficient exam preparation, for example, using study planners, progress trackers, or task management tools to stay organized and focused, reviewing past exam experiences, analyzing mistakes, and learning from feedback can provide valuable insights for future exam attempts, candidates should reflect on their exam performance, identify areas for improvement, and adjust their study strategies accordingly, for example, reviewing exam results, analyzing missed questions, and updating study materials based on feedback, maintaining a growth mindset, embracing challenges, and persevering through setbacks are essential for achieving success in certification exams, candidates should approach exam preparation with a positive attitude, resilience, and determination to overcome obstacles and achieve their goals, for example, reframing setbacks as learning opportunities, seeking feedback, and persisting in the face of challenges.

BOOK 2
ANALYZING VULNERABILITIES
TECHNIQUES AND TOOLS FOR CYSA+ EXAM CS0-003

ROB BOTWRIGHT

Chapter 1: Understanding Vulnerability Assessment

The importance of vulnerability assessment cannot be overstated in today's cybersecurity landscape, vulnerability assessment is a critical process for identifying, evaluating, and mitigating security weaknesses and potential risks within an organization's IT infrastructure, for example, using vulnerability scanning tools such as Nessus, OpenVAS, or Qualys to identify vulnerabilities in network devices, servers, and applications, vulnerability assessment helps organizations proactively identify security vulnerabilities before they can be exploited by attackers, enabling timely remediation and risk reduction, for example, conducting regular vulnerability scans and assessments to identify and prioritize security vulnerabilities based on their severity and impact, vulnerability assessment plays a crucial role in maintaining compliance with regulatory requirements and industry standards, for example, conducting vulnerability assessments to comply with regulatory mandates such as the Payment Card Industry Data Security Standard (PCI DSS) and the Health Insurance Portability and Accountability Act (HIPAA), vulnerability assessment provides valuable insights into the security posture of an organization's IT environment, helping organizations understand their security strengths and weaknesses, for example, using vulnerability assessment reports to identify common security misconfigurations, outdated software versions, and known vulnerabilities, vulnerability assessment helps organizations prioritize remediation efforts and allocate resources effectively to address the most critical security vulnerabilities, for example, using risk-based prioritization techniques to focus on vulnerabilities with the highest potential impact and likelihood of exploitation, vulnerability assessment helps organizations reduce the risk of data breaches, financial losses, and reputational damage associated with security vulnerabilities, for example, patching known vulnerabilities and implementing security controls to mitigate risks, vulnerability assessment is an essential component of a comprehensive cybersecurity strategy, helping organizations identify and address security vulnerabilities across their IT infrastructure, for example, integrating vulnerability assessment into incident response planning, security monitoring, and risk management processes, vulnerability assessment enables organizations to make informed decisions about security investments, priorities, and strategies, for example, using vulnerability assessment reports to justify budget allocations for security initiatives and investments, vulnerability assessment helps organizations demonstrate due diligence and accountability in managing cybersecurity risks, for example, documenting vulnerability assessment activities and remediation efforts to provide evidence of compliance with regulatory requirements and industry best practices, vulnerability assessment enables organizations to stay ahead of emerging threats and evolving security risks, for example, conducting vulnerability assessments regularly to identify new vulnerabilities introduced by software updates, configuration changes, or emerging threats, vulnerability assessment supports continuous improvement and optimization of an organization's security posture, for example, using vulnerability assessment results to identify recurring issues, root causes, and trends for proactive risk mitigation, vulnerability assessment helps organizations build resilience against cyber attacks and security breaches, for example, implementing proactive security measures and controls to prevent, detect, and respond to security threats, vulnerability assessment empowers organizations to take proactive steps to protect their assets, safeguard sensitive information, and maintain trust with customers, partners, and stakeholders, for example, implementing security awareness training, access controls, and encryption to reduce the likelihood and impact of security breaches, vulnerability assessment is an ongoing process that requires regular monitoring, updates, and adaptation to changing threats and technologies, for example, reviewing and updating vulnerability assessment procedures, tools, and methodologies to ensure effectiveness and relevance. Vulnerability scanning tools and techniques are essential components of a robust cybersecurity program, vulnerability scanning involves the automated discovery and assessment of security vulnerabilities within an organization's IT infrastructure, for example, using tools such as Nessus, OpenVAS, or Qualys to scan networks, servers, and applications for known vulnerabilities, vulnerability scanning helps organizations identify and prioritize security weaknesses before they can be exploited by attackers, enabling timely remediation and risk reduction, for example, conducting regular vulnerability scans to identify and address vulnerabilities in a timely manner, vulnerability scanning provides valuable insights into the security posture of an organization's IT environment, helping organizations understand their exposure to potential threats and vulnerabilities, for example, generating vulnerability reports to identify common security misconfigurations, outdated software versions, and known vulnerabilities, vulnerability scanning helps organizations comply with regulatory requirements and industry standards by identifying and addressing security vulnerabilities, for example, conducting vulnerability scans to comply with mandates such as the Payment Card Industry Data Security Standard (PCI DSS) and the Health Insurance Portability and Accountability Act (HIPAA), vulnerability scanning is an integral part of the vulnerability management process, helping organizations assess, prioritize, and remediate security vulnerabilities effectively, for example, integrating vulnerability scanning into incident response planning, security monitoring, and risk management processes, vulnerability scanning enables organizations to detect and remediate security vulnerabilities across their IT infrastructure, for example, using vulnerability scanning tools to identify vulnerabilities in network devices, servers, and applications, vulnerability scanning helps organizations prioritize remediation efforts and allocate resources effectively to address the most critical security vulnerabilities, for example, using risk-based prioritization techniques to focus on vulnerabilities with the highest potential impact and likelihood of exploitation, vulnerability scanning supports continuous improvement and optimization of an organization's security posture, for example, using vulnerability scanning results to identify recurring issues, root causes, and trends for proactive risk mitigation, vulnerability scanning helps organizations reduce the risk of data breaches, financial losses, and reputational damage associated with security vulnerabilities, for example, patching known vulnerabilities and implementing security controls to mitigate risks, vulnerability scanning enables organizations to stay ahead of emerging threats and evolving security risks, for example, conducting vulnerability scans regularly to identify new vulnerabilities introduced by software updates, configuration changes, or emerging threats, vulnerability scanning empowers organizations to make informed decisions about security investments, priorities, and strategies, for example, using vulnerability scanning reports to justify budget allocations for security initiatives and investments, vulnerability scanning helps organizations demonstrate due diligence and accountability in managing cybersecurity risks, for example, documenting vulnerability scanning activities and remediation efforts to provide evidence of compliance with regulatory requirements and industry best practices, vulnerability scanning is an ongoing process that requires regular monitoring, updates, and adaptation to changing threats and technologies, for example, reviewing and updating vulnerability scanning procedures, tools, and methodologies to ensure effectiveness and relevance, vulnerability scanning enables organizations to build resilience against cyber attacks and security breaches, for example, implementing proactive security measures and controls to prevent, detect, and respond to security threats.

Chapter 2: Scanning and Enumeration Techniques

Network scanning methods are fundamental techniques used to discover and analyze devices, services, and vulnerabilities within a network infrastructure, network scanning plays a crucial role in identifying potential security risks and weaknesses, enabling organizations to strengthen their cybersecurity defenses, one of the most common network scanning methods is ICMP (Internet Control Message Protocol) scanning, which involves sending ICMP echo requests to network devices to determine their availability and responsiveness, for example, using the "ping" command in the command-line interface to send ICMP echo requests to a target IP address and receive responses, TCP (Transmission Control Protocol) scanning is another widely used network scanning method that involves sending TCP packets to target ports on network devices to determine their state, for example, using the "nmap" command to perform a TCP SYN scan to identify open ports on a target system, UDP (User Datagram Protocol) scanning is used to identify UDP services running on network devices by sending UDP packets to target ports and analyzing responses, for example, using the "nmap" command with the "-sU" option to perform a UDP scan and identify open UDP ports, banner grabbing is a network scanning technique used to gather information about network services and software versions running on target systems, for example, using the "telnet" command to connect to a target port and retrieve the banner information, OS fingerprinting is a network scanning method used to identify the operating system running on target systems by analyzing network responses and behavior, for example, using the "nmap" command with the "-O" option to perform OS fingerprinting and identify the operating system of a target system, network topology mapping is a network scanning technique used to discover and visualize the layout of network devices and connections, for example, using the "traceroute" command to trace the route packets take from the source to the destination and map network paths, vulnerability scanning is a network scanning method used to identify security vulnerabilities and weaknesses within a network infrastructure, for example, using vulnerability scanning tools such as Nessus or OpenVAS to scan network devices for known vulnerabilities, port scanning is a network scanning technique used to identify open ports and services running on network devices, for example, using the "nmap" command with various scan types such as TCP SYN scan, TCP connect scan, or UDP scan to identify open ports on target systems, network scanning can be performed using both active and passive techniques, with active scanning involving sending probes or requests to target systems and passive scanning involving monitoring network traffic for information, network scanning can also be classified based on the scope of the scan, with internal scanning focusing on scanning devices within an organization's internal network and external scanning focusing on scanning devices accessible from the internet, network scanning is an essential component of network security assessments, audits, and penetration testing activities, enabling organizations to identify and mitigate security risks and vulnerabilities, network scanning should be performed regularly as part of a proactive security strategy to ensure the ongoing protection of network assets and data, network scanning should be conducted in a controlled and authorized manner to avoid disrupting network operations or violating privacy and compliance requirements, network scanning results should be carefully analyzed and interpreted to prioritize remediation efforts and address critical security issues, network scanning tools and techniques should be kept up-to-date to effectively detect and respond to emerging security threats and vulnerabilities. Host enumeration techniques are essential procedures used to gather information about devices connected to a network, these techniques play a crucial role in network reconnaissance and vulnerability assessment, aiding organizations in understanding their network infrastructure and potential security risks, one common host enumeration technique is ARP (Address Resolution Protocol) scanning, which involves sending ARP requests to determine the IP addresses and MAC addresses of devices within a local network, for example, using the "arp-scan" command to perform ARP scanning and enumerate hosts within a subnet, another host enumeration technique is DNS (Domain Name System) enumeration, which involves querying DNS servers to resolve hostnames and retrieve associated IP addresses, for example, using the "nslookup" or "dig" command to perform DNS queries and enumerate hosts within a domain, SNMP (Simple Network Management Protocol) enumeration is a technique used to gather information about network devices and services using SNMP queries, for example, using the "snmpwalk" command to retrieve information from SNMP-enabled devices and enumerate hosts and services, ICMP (Internet Control Message Protocol) enumeration involves sending ICMP echo requests to network devices to determine their availability and responsiveness, for example, using the "ping" command to send ICMP echo requests and enumerate hosts within a network, TCP (Transmission Control Protocol) enumeration is a technique used to identify active TCP services running on network devices by sending TCP packets to target ports and analyzing responses, for example, using the "nmap" command with the "-sS" option to perform a TCP SYN scan and enumerate open TCP ports, UDP (User Datagram Protocol) enumeration is used to identify active UDP services running on network devices by sending UDP packets to target ports and analyzing responses, for example, using the "nmap" command with the "-sU" option to perform a UDP scan and enumerate open UDP ports, NetBIOS enumeration is a technique used to gather information about Windows-based systems by querying NetBIOS services, for example, using the "nbtstat" command to query NetBIOS services and enumerate hosts within a network, SMB (Server Message Block) enumeration is used to gather information about Windows-based systems by querying SMB services, for example, using the "smbclient" command to connect to SMB shares and enumerate hosts and services, LDAP (Lightweight Directory Access Protocol) enumeration is a technique used to gather information about directory services and user accounts by querying LDAP servers, for example, using the "ldapsearch" command to query LDAP servers and enumerate users and groups, SNMP enumeration is a technique used to gather information about network devices and services using SNMP queries, for example, using the "snmpwalk" command to retrieve information from SNMP-enabled devices and enumerate hosts and services, SMTP (Simple Mail Transfer Protocol) enumeration is used to gather information about email servers and user accounts by querying SMTP servers, for example, using the "telnet" command to connect to an SMTP server and enumerate email addresses, host enumeration techniques should be performed in a controlled and authorized manner to avoid disrupting network operations or violating privacy and compliance requirements, host enumeration results should be carefully analyzed and interpreted to prioritize remediation efforts and address critical security issues, host enumeration tools and techniques should be kept up-to-date to effectively detect and respond to emerging security threats and vulnerabilities.

Chapter 3: Vulnerability Management Strategies

Vulnerability prioritization and remediation are critical processes in cybersecurity management, vulnerability prioritization involves assessing and ranking security vulnerabilities based on their severity, impact, and likelihood of exploitation, for example, using vulnerability assessment tools such as Nessus or OpenVAS to generate vulnerability reports and prioritize vulnerabilities based on their Common Vulnerability Scoring System (CVSS) scores, vulnerability prioritization enables organizations to focus their resources and efforts on addressing the most critical security risks first, for example, creating a risk matrix or scoring system to assign priorities to vulnerabilities based on their potential impact on business operations and data confidentiality, vulnerability prioritization should take into account factors such as the availability of exploit code, the existence of active attacks, and the potential impact on critical systems or data, for example, using threat intelligence feeds and security advisories to identify vulnerabilities actively targeted by attackers and prioritize remediation efforts accordingly, vulnerability remediation involves taking steps to address and mitigate security vulnerabilities identified through vulnerability assessments, for example, applying software patches, implementing configuration changes, or deploying security controls to reduce the risk of exploitation, vulnerability remediation should be performed promptly and systematically to minimize the window of exposure and reduce the likelihood of successful attacks, for example, establishing a vulnerability management process with defined roles, responsibilities, and timelines for remediating vulnerabilities, prioritizing vulnerabilities based on their severity and potential impact allows organizations to allocate resources effectively and address the most significant security risks first, for example, creating a remediation plan with specific actions, deadlines, and escalation procedures for addressing high-priority vulnerabilities, vulnerability prioritization and remediation should be integrated into the organization's overall risk management and cybersecurity strategy, for example, aligning vulnerability management activities with business objectives, compliance requirements, and risk tolerance levels, vulnerability prioritization should involve collaboration between different stakeholders, including IT teams, security professionals, and business leaders, for example, conducting regular vulnerability review meetings to discuss findings, assign priorities, and track remediation progress, automated vulnerability management tools can streamline the prioritization and remediation process by providing real-time visibility into the organization's security posture and automating routine tasks, for example, using vulnerability management platforms such as Rapid7 InsightVM or Tenable.io to scan, prioritize, and remediate vulnerabilities across the enterprise, continuous monitoring and reassessment of vulnerabilities are essential to ensure that remediation efforts are effective and sustainable, for example, implementing a continuous monitoring program to detect new vulnerabilities, track remediation progress, and assess the effectiveness of security controls, organizations should establish metrics and key performance indicators (KPIs) to measure the effectiveness of their vulnerability prioritization and remediation efforts, for example, tracking metrics such as time to remediate, percentage of critical vulnerabilities patched, and reduction in overall risk exposure, vulnerability prioritization and remediation are ongoing processes that require regular review and adjustment to address emerging threats and changing business requirements, for example, conducting periodic vulnerability assessments, reviewing remediation progress, and updating risk management policies and procedures accordingly. Patch management best practices are essential for maintaining the security and integrity of IT systems, patch management involves the process of identifying, deploying, and managing software updates, or patches, to address security vulnerabilities and improve system performance, for example, using patch management tools such as WSUS (Windows Server Update Services) or SCCM (System Center Configuration Manager) to centrally deploy patches to Windows systems, organizations should establish a patch management policy and procedure to define roles, responsibilities, and workflows for managing patches across the enterprise, for example, creating a patch management policy document that outlines the patching process, patch deployment schedule, and criteria for prioritizing patches, patch management should begin with vulnerability assessment to identify and prioritize security vulnerabilities that require patching, for example, using vulnerability scanning tools such as Nessus or OpenVAS to scan systems for known vulnerabilities, organizations should prioritize patches based on their severity, impact, and exploitability to address the most critical security risks first, for example, using the Common Vulnerability Scoring System (CVSS) to assess and prioritize patches based on their CVSS scores, patches should be tested in a non-production environment before deployment to ensure compatibility and minimize the risk of system downtime or disruption, for example, creating a test environment that mirrors the production environment and deploying patches to test systems before rolling them out to production, organizations should schedule regular patch deployment windows to ensure timely patching of systems and minimize the window of exposure to security vulnerabilities, for example, establishing a monthly patch deployment schedule with predefined maintenance windows for applying patches to production systems, patches should be deployed using automated patch management tools to streamline the process and ensure consistency across the organization, for example, using batch scripts or PowerShell commands to automate patch deployment tasks, organizations should monitor patch deployment status and track compliance with patch management policies and procedures, for example, using patch management tools to generate reports and dashboards that provide visibility into patching activities and compliance status, patch management should include processes for rollback and remediation in case of patch-related issues or system failures, for example, creating backup and recovery procedures to restore systems to a previous state in the event of patch-related problems, organizations should establish a communication plan to notify stakeholders about upcoming patch deployments, maintenance windows, and system downtime, for example, sending email notifications, posting announcements on intranet portals, or scheduling meetings to inform stakeholders about patching activities, patch management should be integrated into the organization's overall risk management and cybersecurity strategy to ensure alignment with business objectives and compliance requirements, for example, conducting regular risk assessments to identify and prioritize patching activities based on their impact on business operations and data security, organizations should keep patch management tools and processes up-to-date to effectively detect and respond to emerging threats and vulnerabilities, for example, regularly updating patch management software and procedures to support new platforms, applications, and security patches, patch management is an ongoing process that requires continuous monitoring, evaluation, and improvement to address evolving security threats and changing business requirements, for example, conducting post-implementation reviews and lessons learned sessions to identify areas for improvement and optimize patch management practices.

Chapter 4: Exploitation Frameworks and Tools

Introduction to exploitation frameworks provides an overview of powerful tools and platforms used by cybersecurity professionals and attackers alike to discover and exploit vulnerabilities in target systems, one of the most widely used exploitation frameworks is Metasploit, an open-source framework that provides a comprehensive suite of tools for penetration testing, vulnerability assessment, and exploit development, for example, using the "msfconsole" command to launch the Metasploit console and access its features, Metasploit includes a vast library of pre-built exploits, payloads, and auxiliary modules that can be used to test and exploit security vulnerabilities in target systems, for example, using the "search" command to search for available exploits and modules within Metasploit, Metasploit simplifies the process of exploiting vulnerabilities by providing automated exploitation techniques, for example, using the "use" command to select an exploit module and the "exploit" command to launch the exploit against a target system, Metasploit also includes post-exploitation modules for performing tasks such as privilege escalation, lateral movement, and data exfiltration, for example, using the "post" command to access post-exploitation modules and perform further actions on compromised systems, another popular exploitation framework is Cobalt Strike, a commercial platform used by penetration testers and red teamers to simulate advanced persistent threat (APT) attacks and perform targeted exploitation campaigns, for example, using the "beacon" command to establish a command-and-control (C2) channel with compromised systems and execute commands remotely, Cobalt Strike includes features such as beaconing, phishing, and social engineering to simulate real-world attack scenarios and test defensive capabilities, for example, using the "spearphish" command to launch targeted phishing campaigns and lure users into clicking malicious links or downloading payloads, Cobalt Strike also supports the development and customization of custom exploits and payloads using its built-in scripting language, for example, using the "script" command to write and execute custom scripts for automating tasks or extending Cobalt Strike's functionality, other exploitation frameworks include Canvas, Core Impact, and Empire, each with its own set of features, capabilities, and use cases, for example, using the "canvas" command to launch Canvas and access its graphical user interface (GUI) for exploiting vulnerabilities, exploitation frameworks are powerful tools that can be used for both offensive and defensive purposes, enabling cybersecurity professionals to test and validate the effectiveness of security controls and measures, for example, using exploitation frameworks to identify and patch vulnerabilities before they can be exploited by attackers, exploitation frameworks should be used responsibly and ethically in accordance with legal and ethical guidelines, for example, ensuring that exploitation activities are conducted with proper authorization and consent from stakeholders, exploitation frameworks require continuous updating and maintenance to keep pace with emerging threats and vulnerabilities, for example, regularly updating exploitation frameworks and modules to incorporate new exploits, payloads, and techniques, exploitation frameworks are valuable resources for cybersecurity professionals seeking to improve their skills and knowledge of offensive security techniques, for example, participating in training courses, workshops, and capture-the-flag (CTF) competitions to learn and practice using exploitation frameworks effectively. Exploitation techniques and mitigation strategies are vital components of cybersecurity defense strategies aimed at protecting systems and networks from malicious attacks, understanding common exploitation techniques is essential for security professionals to develop effective mitigation strategies and safeguards against potential threats, one prevalent exploitation technique is buffer overflow attacks, which involve sending more data to a program buffer than it can handle, resulting in the execution of arbitrary code or the crashing of the program, for example, using the "buffer overflow" command to execute a buffer overflow attack against a vulnerable application, mitigation strategies for buffer overflow attacks include input validation, bounds checking, and stack canaries to detect and prevent buffer overflow vulnerabilities, for example, implementing input sanitization routines and using programming languages with built-in memory protections such as stack cookies or Address Space Layout Randomization (ASLR), another common exploitation technique is SQL injection, which involves inserting malicious SQL code into input fields to manipulate databases and extract sensitive information, for example, using the "sqlmap" command to automate SQL injection attacks and identify vulnerable web applications, mitigation strategies for SQL injection attacks include input validation, parameterized queries, and database permissions to restrict access and prevent unauthorized SQL queries, for example, using prepared statements and stored procedures to sanitize input data and enforce least privilege access controls, cross-site scripting (XSS) is another prevalent exploitation technique that involves injecting malicious scripts into web pages viewed by other users, for example, using the "xss" command to execute XSS attacks and steal session cookies or sensitive information from users, mitigation strategies for XSS attacks include input validation, output encoding, and content security policies to prevent the execution of malicious scripts, for example, using HTML escaping libraries and enforcing strict content security policies to block inline scripts and limit the execution of external scripts, privilege escalation is a common exploitation technique used to gain unauthorized access to privileged accounts or system resources, for example, using the "sudo" command to escalate privileges and execute commands with root privileges, mitigation strategies for privilege escalation attacks include least privilege access controls, strong authentication mechanisms, and system hardening to limit the impact of potential exploits, for example, configuring user accounts with minimal privileges and implementing multi-factor authentication (MFA) to verify user identities, denial-of-service (DoS) and distributed denial-of-service (DDoS) attacks are exploitation techniques aimed at disrupting the availability of network services by overwhelming target systems with excessive traffic or resource requests, for example, using the "hping" command to launch DoS attacks and flood target systems with ICMP or UDP packets, mitigation strategies for DoS and DDoS attacks include traffic filtering, rate limiting, and network segmentation to mitigate the impact of attack traffic and maintain service availability, for example, deploying firewalls, intrusion detection systems (IDS), and load balancers to filter and manage incoming traffic, exploitation techniques are continuously evolving as attackers develop new methods and tactics to bypass security defenses and exploit vulnerabilities, for example, using machine learning algorithms and anomaly detection techniques to identify and block suspicious behavior and patterns, mitigation strategies should be regularly reviewed and updated to address emerging threats and vulnerabilities, for example, conducting regular security assessments and penetration tests to identify weaknesses and validate the effectiveness of mitigation measures, collaboration and information sharing among security professionals are essential for staying informed about new exploitation techniques and best practices for mitigation, for example, participating in threat intelligence sharing communities, security conferences, and industry forums to exchange knowledge and insights about emerging threats and attack trends.

Chapter 5: Web Application Security Assessment

Common web application vulnerabilities pose significant risks to the security and integrity of web-based systems, understanding these vulnerabilities is crucial for developers, security professionals, and system administrators to implement effective mitigation strategies and protect against potential attacks, one prevalent web application vulnerability is SQL injection, which allows attackers to manipulate SQL queries through user input fields, potentially leading to unauthorized access to databases or sensitive information, for example, using tools like SQLMap to automate SQL injection attacks and exploit vulnerable web applications, mitigation strategies for SQL injection include input validation, parameterized queries, and using ORM (Object-Relational Mapping) libraries to prevent attackers from injecting malicious SQL code, another common web application vulnerability is cross-site scripting (XSS), where attackers inject malicious scripts into web pages viewed by other users, enabling them to steal session cookies, redirect users to malicious websites, or deface web pages, for example, using tools like Burp Suite to detect and exploit XSS vulnerabilities in web applications, mitigation strategies for XSS vulnerabilities include input validation, output encoding, and implementing strict content security policies to prevent the execution of malicious scripts, insecure direct object references occur when web applications expose internal file or database resources without proper authorization checks, allowing attackers to manipulate URLs or parameters to access unauthorized data, for example, using tools like OWASP ZAP to identify and exploit insecure direct object references in web applications, mitigation strategies for insecure direct object references include access controls, session management, and using unique identifiers to reference sensitive data instead of predictable values, cross-site request forgery (CSRF) is a web application vulnerability that allows attackers to trick authenticated users into performing unintended actions on a web application, for example, using tools like CSRFTester to simulate CSRF attacks and exploit vulnerabilities in web applications, mitigation strategies for CSRF vulnerabilities include using anti-CSRF tokens, validating request origins, and implementing strict referer policies to prevent attackers from forging requests, security misconfiguration is a common web application vulnerability that occurs when systems are not securely configured or hardened, leaving them vulnerable to attacks such as directory traversal, unauthorized access, or information disclosure, for example, using tools like Nikto to identify security misconfigurations and vulnerabilities in web servers, mitigation strategies for security misconfigurations include regularly updating software, disabling unnecessary services, and implementing security best practices such as using strong passwords and encryption, insufficient logging and monitoring is a web application vulnerability that can allow attackers to exploit security weaknesses and evade detection by security controls, for example, using tools like Log4j to identify and exploit insufficient logging and monitoring vulnerabilities in web applications, mitigation strategies for insufficient logging and monitoring include implementing robust logging mechanisms, monitoring logs for suspicious activity, and using intrusion detection systems (IDS) and security information and event management (SIEM) tools to detect and respond to security incidents, broken authentication occurs when web applications fail to properly authenticate and manage user sessions, allowing attackers to hijack user accounts, impersonate users, or escalate privileges, for example, using tools like Hydra to launch brute force attacks and exploit vulnerabilities in web application authentication mechanisms, mitigation strategies for broken authentication include using strong passwords, implementing multi-factor authentication (MFA), and enforcing session timeouts to reduce the risk of unauthorized access, vulnerable components such as libraries, frameworks, and plugins used in web applications can introduce security vulnerabilities if not properly managed and updated, for example, using tools like Retire.js to identify vulnerable components and dependencies in web applications, mitigation strategies for vulnerable components include regularly updating software, monitoring for security advisories and patches, and using tools like dependency checkers to identify and remediate vulnerabilities, XML external entity (XXE) injection is a web application vulnerability that occurs when XML parsers process external entities, allowing attackers to read sensitive data, execute remote code, or perform denial-of-service attacks, for example, using tools like XXEinjector to identify and exploit XXE vulnerabilities in web applications, mitigation strategies for XXE vulnerabilities include disabling external entity processing, validating XML input, and using XML parsers that are not vulnerable to XXE attacks, insecure deserialization is a web application vulnerability that occurs when serialized data is manipulated by attackers to execute arbitrary code or perform unauthorized actions, for example, using tools like ysoserial to exploit insecure deserialization vulnerabilities in web applications, mitigation strategies for insecure deserialization include input validation, using secure serialization formats, and implementing strict access controls to prevent attackers from exploiting deserialization vulnerabilities. Web application security testing methodologies are crucial for ensuring the robustness and resilience of web-based systems against various cyber threats and vulnerabilities, these methodologies encompass a range of techniques and approaches designed to identify and address security weaknesses in web applications, one commonly used methodology is the OWASP (Open Web Application Security Project) testing guide, which provides a comprehensive framework for conducting web application security assessments, for example, using tools like OWASP ZAP (Zed Attack Proxy) to perform automated security scans and identify vulnerabilities in web applications, the OWASP testing guide covers a wide range of security testing techniques, including reconnaissance, mapping, discovery, and exploitation, for example, using the "zap-cli" command to run OWASP ZAP scans from the command line interface, another widely adopted methodology is the PTES (Penetration Testing Execution Standard), which outlines a systematic approach to conducting penetration tests against web applications, for example, using tools like Burp Suite to perform manual security testing and identify vulnerabilities in web applications, the PTES methodology involves several phases, including pre-engagement, intelligence gathering, threat modeling, vulnerability analysis, and reporting, for example, using the "burp" command to launch Burp Suite and initiate security assessments against web applications, the PTES methodology emphasizes the importance of collaboration between security professionals, developers, and stakeholders throughout the testing process, for example, using collaboration tools like JIRA or Slack to communicate findings, track remediation progress, and coordinate security efforts, other web application security testing methodologies include the NIST (National Institute of Standards and Technology) SP 800-115 framework, which provides guidance on conducting technical security assessments of web applications, for example, using tools like Nikto to perform web server vulnerability scans and identify security weaknesses, the NIST SP 800-115 framework emphasizes the need for thorough documentation, risk assessment, and validation of findings during the testing process, for example, using tools like Dradis to document security assessment results and generate comprehensive reports for stakeholders, regardless of the methodology used, web application security testing should be conducted regularly and systematically to identify and mitigate potential security risks, for example, using tools like Jenkins or GitLab CI/CD pipelines to automate security testing as part of the software development lifecycle, continuous integration and continuous deployment (CI/CD) pipelines enable organizations to integrate security testing into the software development process and identify vulnerabilities early in the development lifecycle, for example, using tools like SonarQube to perform static code analysis and identify security vulnerabilities in web application source code, integrating security testing into CI/CD pipelines helps organizations detect and remediate vulnerabilities quickly, reducing the risk of security incidents and data breaches, for example, using tools like OWASP Dependency-Check to scan software dependencies for known vulnerabilities and ensure that third-party libraries are free from security flaws, in addition to automated testing, manual security testing by skilled professionals is essential for identifying complex security vulnerabilities and ensuring the effectiveness of security controls, for example, using tools like OWASP WebGoat to practice manual security testing techniques and learn about common web application vulnerabilities, leveraging both automated and manual testing techniques allows organizations to comprehensively assess the security posture of their web applications and prioritize remediation efforts based on risk and impact, for example, using tools like OWASP Juice Shop to simulate real-world web application security vulnerabilities and practice exploit techniques in a safe and controlled environment, organizations should also consider engaging external security experts or penetration testing firms to conduct independent security assessments and provide objective insights into the security posture of their web applications, for example, hiring certified ethical hackers or penetration testers to perform black-box, white-box, or gray-box testing against web applications and identify security vulnerabilities from an attacker's perspective, collaborating with external security experts can help organizations uncover hidden vulnerabilities and strengthen their overall security posture, for example, using tools like OWASP Amass to perform DNS enumeration and discover subdomains associated with web applications, proactive security testing and continuous improvement are essential for staying ahead of evolving cyber threats and maintaining the security and integrity of web-based systems.

Chapter 6: Network Penetration Testing

Network penetration testing is a systematic process used to evaluate the security of a network infrastructure by simulating real-world attacks and identifying vulnerabilities that could be exploited by malicious actors, one crucial aspect of the network penetration testing process is reconnaissance, which involves gathering information about the target network, including IP addresses, domain names, network topology, and system configurations, for example, using tools like Nmap to scan the target network and discover open ports, services, and hosts, reconnaissance helps penetration testers understand the scope and complexity of the target network and identify potential entry points for exploitation, another key phase of the network penetration testing process is enumeration, which involves actively probing the target network to gather additional information about its systems, services, and users, for example, using tools like enum4linux to enumerate Windows systems and extract information such as user accounts, shares, and group memberships, enumeration helps penetration testers identify potential vulnerabilities and misconfigurations that could be leveraged to gain unauthorized access to network resources, vulnerability scanning is another critical component of the network penetration testing process, which involves using automated tools to scan the target network for known security vulnerabilities and weaknesses, for example, using tools like Nessus or OpenVAS to perform vulnerability scans and identify missing patches, misconfigurations, or insecure protocols, vulnerability scanning helps penetration testers prioritize remediation efforts and focus on addressing critical security issues that pose the greatest risk to the target network, exploitation is a core aspect of the network penetration testing process, which involves leveraging identified vulnerabilities to gain unauthorized access to network resources, escalate privileges, or execute arbitrary code, for example, using tools like Metasploit to exploit known vulnerabilities and compromise target systems, exploitation helps penetration testers demonstrate the potential impact of security vulnerabilities and provide recommendations for improving the security posture of the target network, post-exploitation is a crucial phase of the network penetration testing process, which involves maintaining access to compromised systems, conducting further reconnaissance, and exfiltrating sensitive information, for example, using tools like PowerShell Empire or Cobalt Strike to establish persistent access to compromised systems and exfiltrate data, post-exploitation activities help penetration testers assess the effectiveness of security controls and identify additional security weaknesses that could be exploited by attackers, reporting is the final phase of the network penetration testing process, which involves documenting findings, vulnerabilities, and recommendations in a comprehensive report for stakeholders, for example, using tools like Dradis to generate professional-looking penetration test reports and communicate findings effectively, reporting helps penetration testers convey the results of the penetration test to management, IT teams, and other relevant stakeholders and provide actionable recommendations for improving the security posture of the target network, continuous improvement is essential for the network penetration testing process, as new vulnerabilities and attack techniques emerge, for example, using tools like GitLab or JIRA to track remediation efforts and ensure that security vulnerabilities are addressed in a timely manner, continuous improvement helps organizations enhance their security defenses and mitigate the risk of future security incidents or data breaches, collaboration and communication are crucial aspects of the network penetration testing process, as penetration testers work closely with IT teams, system administrators, and other stakeholders to assess the security posture of the target network and identify potential security risks, for example, using tools like Slack or Microsoft Teams to facilitate collaboration, communication helps penetration testers share findings, coordinate remediation efforts, and ensure that security vulnerabilities are addressed effectively, adherence to industry standards and best practices is important for the network penetration testing process, as it helps ensure that penetration tests are conducted ethically, thoroughly, and in accordance with legal and regulatory requirements, for example, following guidelines outlined in industry frameworks such as the Penetration Testing Execution Standard (PTES) or the NIST Special Publication 800-115, adherence to industry standards and best practices helps organizations demonstrate due diligence and compliance with relevant regulations, standards, and frameworks, for example, using tools like Burp Suite or OWASP ZAP to perform web application penetration tests and identify vulnerabilities in web-based systems, web application penetration testing helps organizations identify and address security weaknesses in web applications, such as SQL injection, cross-site scripting (XSS), and insecure authentication mechanisms, for example, using tools like Nikto or WPScan to scan web servers and identify security vulnerabilities in web applications, web application penetration testing helps organizations assess the security posture of their web-based systems and identify potential security risks, such as insecure configurations, vulnerabilities, or misconfigurations, for example, using tools like SQLMap or sqlninja to automate SQL injection attacks and exploit vulnerabilities in web applications, web application penetration testing helps organizations identify and remediate security vulnerabilities in web-based systems, reducing the risk of data breaches, unauthorized access, or other security incidents, for example, using tools like Burp Suite or OWASP ZAP to perform manual security testing and identify vulnerabilities in web applications, manual security testing helps organizations uncover complex security vulnerabilities that may not be detected by automated scanning tools, such as business logic flaws, for example, using tools like Nessus or OpenVAS to perform vulnerability scans and identify security weaknesses in network devices, network penetration testing helps organizations assess the security posture of their network infrastructure and identify potential security risks, such as misconfigurations, vulnerabilities, or insecure protocols, for example, using tools like Metasploit or Cobalt Strike to exploit known vulnerabilities and compromise target systems, network penetration testing helps organizations understand the potential impact of security vulnerabilities and prioritize remediation efforts, for example, using tools like PowerShell Empire or Meterpreter to establish persistent access to compromised systems and exfiltrate sensitive information, post-exploitation activities help organizations assess the effectiveness of their security controls and identify additional security weaknesses, for example, using tools like Dradis or ReportPortal to generate professional-looking penetration test reports and communicate findings effectively, reporting helps organizations convey the results of penetration tests to management, IT teams, and other relevant stakeholders, for example, using tools like GitLab or JIRA to track remediation efforts and ensure that security vulnerabilities are addressed in a timely manner, continuous improvement helps organizations enhance their security defenses and mitigate the risk of future security incidents or data breaches. Post-exploitation techniques are a critical aspect of cybersecurity assessments, allowing penetration testers to maintain access to compromised systems, gather additional information, and demonstrate the potential impact of security vulnerabilities, one common post-exploitation technique is establishing persistent access to compromised systems using backdoors or remote access trojans (RATs), for example, using tools like Metasploit or Cobalt Strike to deploy a Meterpreter payload and establish a reverse shell connection to the compromised system, establishing persistent access allows penetration testers to maintain control over compromised systems even after the initial exploitation phase, enabling them to conduct further reconnaissance, escalate privileges, or exfiltrate sensitive data, another post-exploitation technique is privilege escalation, which involves gaining additional privileges on compromised systems to access restricted resources or execute privileged commands, for example, using tools like Windows Exploit Suggester to identify potential privilege escalation vulnerabilities in Windows systems, privilege escalation techniques may exploit misconfigured permissions, weak service configurations, or known vulnerabilities to elevate privileges and gain access to sensitive information, lateral movement is another important post-exploitation technique, which involves moving laterally across a network to access additional systems or resources, for example, using tools like BloodHound or CrackMapExec to identify and exploit trust relationships, weak credentials, or misconfigured network shares to move laterally within a network, lateral movement techniques allow penetration testers to expand their foothold within a network and access critical systems or data, data exfiltration is a key post-exploitation activity, which involves stealing and exfiltrating sensitive information from compromised systems, for example, using tools like FTP or SCP to transfer files from compromised systems to an external server controlled by the penetration tester, data exfiltration techniques may involve compressing, encrypting, or obfuscating stolen data to evade detection and maintain stealth, post-exploitation activities should be conducted carefully and ethically to avoid causing damage or disruption to the target environment, for example, using tools like PowerShell Empire or Cobalt Strike to simulate data exfiltration and assess the effectiveness of security controls, stealth and persistence are essential considerations when conducting post-exploitation activities, as attackers aim to maintain access to compromised systems while avoiding detection by security defenses, for example, using techniques like living-off-the-land (LOLBin) or fileless malware to execute commands or manipulate system configurations without leaving traces, reporting is a critical aspect of post-exploitation activities, allowing penetration testers to document findings, vulnerabilities, and recommendations in a comprehensive report for stakeholders, for example, using tools like Dradis or ReportPortal to generate professional-looking penetration test reports and communicate findings effectively, reporting helps penetration testers convey the results of post-exploitation activities to management, IT teams, and other relevant stakeholders, providing actionable recommendations for improving the security posture of the target environment, transparency and accountability are important principles when conducting post-exploitation activities, as penetration testers must ensure that their actions are well-documented and justified, for example, using tools like JIRA or GitLab to track post-exploitation activities and ensure that remediation efforts are prioritized and addressed in a timely manner, collaboration and communication are essential during the post-exploitation phase, as penetration testers work closely with IT teams, system administrators, and other stakeholders to address security vulnerabilities and mitigate risks, for example, using tools like Slack or Microsoft Teams to facilitate collaboration and communication, post-exploitation activities should be conducted in accordance with industry standards and best practices, ensuring that ethical guidelines and legal requirements are followed, for example, adhering to guidelines outlined in industry frameworks such as the Penetration Testing Execution Standard (PTES) or the NIST Special Publication 800-115, continuous improvement is important for post-exploitation activities, as new vulnerabilities and attack techniques emerge, for example, using tools like OWASP Juice Shop or Damn Vulnerable Web Application (DVWA) to practice post-exploitation techniques and enhance skills, continuous improvement helps penetration testers stay up-to-date with evolving threats and maintain proficiency in conducting post-exploitation activities, for example, using tools like OWASP Amass or Sublist3r to perform DNS enumeration and discover subdomains associated with the target environment, proactive post-exploitation activities can help organizations identify and remediate security vulnerabilities before they are exploited by malicious actors, for example, using tools like BeEF (Browser Exploitation Framework) to simulate client-side attacks and assess the security posture of web applications, proactive post-exploitation activities complement traditional security assessments and help organizations identify blind spots or overlooked security risks, for example, using tools like Responder or mitmproxy to intercept and manipulate network traffic, enabling penetration testers to identify security weaknesses in network protocols or applications, proactive post-exploitation activities are essential for organizations to maintain a proactive security posture and prevent potential security incidents or data breaches.

Chapter 7: Wireless Network Security Analysis

Wireless network security risks pose significant challenges for organizations, as wireless networks are inherently more vulnerable to attacks due to their broadcast nature and reliance on radio waves for communication, one of the primary risks associated with wireless networks is unauthorized access, which occurs when attackers gain unauthorized access to a wireless network without proper authentication, for example, using tools like Aircrack-ng or Wireshark to capture and analyze wireless network traffic, unauthorized access can lead to data theft, unauthorized use of network resources, or disruption of network services, another risk is eavesdropping, which occurs when attackers intercept and monitor wireless network traffic to capture sensitive information, such as passwords, credit card numbers, or confidential business data, for example, using tools like Kismet or Wireshark to sniff wireless network traffic and capture data packets, eavesdropping can compromise the confidentiality and integrity of transmitted data, exposing organizations to data breaches and privacy violations, rogue access points are another common risk associated with wireless networks, which occurs when unauthorized wireless access points are deployed within the vicinity of a corporate network, for example, using tools like NetStumbler or Airodump-ng to detect rogue access points and identify unauthorized devices connected to the network, rogue access points can be used by attackers to launch man-in-the-middle (MitM) attacks, distribute malware, or steal sensitive information, denial-of-service (DoS) attacks are a significant risk for wireless networks, which occurs when attackers flood a wireless network with malicious traffic to disrupt normal network operations, for example, using tools like MDK3 or aireplay-ng to launch deauthentication or disassociation attacks against wireless clients or access points, DoS attacks can degrade network performance, interrupt critical services, or cause network outages, encryption weaknesses are another risk associated with wireless networks, as many wireless security protocols, such as WEP (Wired Equivalent Privacy) or WPA (Wi-Fi Protected Access), have known vulnerabilities that can be exploited by attackers to bypass encryption and gain unauthorized access to the network, for example, using tools like Aircrack-ng or Reaver to crack WEP or WPA/WPA2 encryption keys and compromise wireless networks, encryption weaknesses can expose sensitive data to interception, tampering, or unauthorized access, insecure configuration is a significant risk for wireless networks, as misconfigured wireless routers, access points, or client devices may expose network services, sensitive information, or administrative interfaces to unauthorized access, for example, using tools like Nmap or Nessus to scan wireless networks for misconfigured devices or insecure services, insecure configurations can result in unauthorized access, data breaches, or network compromise, lack of monitoring and visibility is another risk associated with wireless networks, as organizations may lack visibility into wireless network activity, devices, or security events, for example, using tools like Snort or Suricata to monitor wireless network traffic and detect suspicious or malicious activity, lack of monitoring and visibility can make it difficult for organizations to detect and respond to security incidents in a timely manner, insecure authentication is a significant risk for wireless networks, as weak or default passwords, shared keys, or insecure authentication protocols may be used to authenticate wireless clients or access points, for example, using tools like John the Ripper or Hydra to perform password cracking attacks against wireless networks, insecure authentication mechanisms can compromise the confidentiality and integrity of network communications, exposing organizations to unauthorized access, data breaches, or other security incidents, lack of security awareness and training is another risk associated with wireless networks, as users may lack awareness of security best practices, policies, or procedures for securely configuring and using wireless devices, for example, providing security awareness training to employees on how to identify and report suspicious wireless network activity, lack of security awareness and training can increase the risk of security incidents, data breaches, or compliance violations, securing wireless networks requires a multi-layered approach that addresses the various risks and vulnerabilities associated with wireless technology, for example, implementing strong encryption, authentication, access controls, and monitoring mechanisms to protect wireless networks from unauthorized access, data breaches, or other security incidents, organizations should also conduct regular security assessments, vulnerability scans, and penetration tests to identify and address security weaknesses in wireless networks, for example, using tools like Nessus or OpenVAS to perform vulnerability scans and identify security vulnerabilities in wireless devices, implementing security policies, procedures, and controls that govern the secure configuration, use, and management of wireless devices and networks, for example, using tools like Microsoft NPS (Network Policy Server) or FreeRADIUS to implement network access controls and enforce security policies for wireless clients, organizations should also monitor wireless network traffic, devices, and security events in real-time to detect and respond to security incidents, for example, using tools like Snort or Suricata to monitor wireless network traffic and alert on suspicious or malicious activity, proactive security measures, such as regular software updates, patches, and firmware upgrades, can help mitigate the risk of security vulnerabilities and ensure the security and integrity of wireless networks, for example, using tools like Nmap or Nessus to scan wireless networks for outdated software, insecure configurations, or known vulnerabilities, proactive security measures can help organizations identify and address security weaknesses before they are exploited by attackers. Wireless penetration testing techniques are essential for assessing the security posture of wireless networks and identifying potential vulnerabilities and weaknesses that could be exploited by attackers, one common technique used in wireless penetration testing is wireless network discovery, which involves scanning for available wireless networks and identifying access points, for example, using tools like Airodump-ng or NetStumbler to scan for nearby wireless networks and capture information such as SSIDs, MAC addresses, and signal strength, wireless network discovery helps penetration testers understand the scope and complexity of the target environment and identify potential entry points for exploitation, another technique is wireless network enumeration, which involves gathering additional information about wireless networks, such as connected devices, encryption methods, and security settings, for example, using tools like Kismet or Wireshark to passively monitor wireless network traffic and gather information about connected clients, wireless network enumeration helps penetration testers identify potential security weaknesses and misconfigurations that could be leveraged to gain unauthorized access to the network, wireless network fingerprinting is another technique used in wireless penetration testing, which involves identifying specific characteristics or features of wireless networks, such as vendor-specific information, for example, using tools like Airmon-ng or MAC Changer to manipulate wireless network parameters and gather information about wireless devices and access points, wireless network fingerprinting helps penetration testers identify potential vulnerabilities or security weaknesses that could be exploited during an attack, wireless network sniffing is a critical technique used in wireless penetration testing, which involves capturing and analyzing wireless network traffic to identify potential security vulnerabilities or threats, for example, using tools like Wireshark or Tcpdump to capture wireless network packets and analyze network traffic for signs of suspicious or malicious activity, wireless network sniffing helps penetration testers identify potential security risks, such as unauthorized access, data breaches, or network misuse, wireless network exploitation is a key technique used in wireless penetration testing, which involves exploiting identified vulnerabilities or weaknesses in wireless networks to gain unauthorized access or compromise network resources, for example, using tools like Aircrack-ng or Reaver to crack WEP or WPA/WPA2 encryption keys and gain unauthorized access to a wireless network, wireless network exploitation allows penetration testers to demonstrate the potential impact of security vulnerabilities and provide recommendations for improving the security posture of the target environment, wireless network post-exploitation is another important technique used in wireless penetration testing, which involves maintaining access to compromised wireless networks and conducting further reconnaissance or exfiltrating sensitive information, for example, using tools like Metasploit or Cobalt Strike to establish persistent access to compromised wireless networks and exfiltrate data, wireless network post-exploitation allows penetration testers to assess the effectiveness of security controls and identify additional security weaknesses that could be exploited by attackers, wireless network reporting is a critical aspect of wireless penetration testing, allowing penetration testers to document findings, vulnerabilities, and recommendations in a comprehensive report for stakeholders, for example, using tools like Dradis or ReportPortal to generate professional-looking penetration test reports and communicate findings effectively, wireless network reporting helps penetration testers convey the results of the penetration test to management, IT teams, and other relevant stakeholders and provide actionable recommendations for improving the security posture of the target environment, collaboration and communication are essential during wireless penetration testing, as penetration testers work closely with IT teams, system administrators, and other stakeholders to assess the security posture of wireless networks and identify potential security risks, for example, using tools like Slack or Microsoft Teams to facilitate collaboration and communication, wireless penetration testing should be conducted in accordance with industry standards and best practices, ensuring that ethical guidelines and legal requirements are followed, for example, following guidelines outlined in industry frameworks such as the Penetration Testing Execution Standard (PTES) or the NIST Special Publication 800-115, continuous improvement is important for wireless penetration testing, as new vulnerabilities and attack techniques emerge, for example, using tools like OWASP Juice Shop or Damn Vulnerable Web Application (DVWA) to practice wireless penetration testing techniques and enhance skills, continuous improvement helps penetration testers stay up-to-date with evolving threats and maintain proficiency in conducting wireless penetration testing activities.

Chapter 8: Mobile Device Security Assessment

Mobile device security risks and threats pose significant challenges for individuals and organizations, as mobile devices have become an integral part of daily life and business operations, one of the primary risks associated with mobile devices is data loss or theft, which occurs when sensitive information stored on a mobile device is compromised or accessed by unauthorized parties, for example, using tools like Metasploit or ADB (Android Debug Bridge) to exploit vulnerabilities in mobile operating systems and gain unauthorized access to device data, data loss or theft can result in financial loss, reputational damage, or regulatory penalties, another risk is malware infections, which occur when malicious software is installed on a mobile device without the user's knowledge or consent, for example, using techniques like phishing or social engineering to trick users into downloading and installing malicious apps or software, malware infections can compromise the confidentiality, integrity, and availability of device data and resources, exposing users to identity theft, financial fraud, or unauthorized surveillance, insecure network connections are another common risk associated with mobile devices, as users often connect to public Wi-Fi networks or unsecured hotspots that are vulnerable to interception or eavesdropping, for example, using tools like Wireshark or tcpdump to capture and analyze network traffic on public Wi-Fi networks and intercept sensitive information, insecure network connections can expose users to man-in-the-middle (MitM) attacks, data interception, or session hijacking, insufficient authentication and access controls are significant risks for mobile devices, as many users rely on weak or default passwords, PINs, or biometric authentication methods to protect device access, for example, using tools like John the Ripper or Hashcat to crack weak passwords or brute-force authentication credentials, insufficient authentication and access controls can allow unauthorized users to bypass device security measures and gain access to sensitive information or perform unauthorized actions, inadequate encryption is another risk associated with mobile devices, as many devices lack encryption mechanisms to protect data stored on the device or transmitted over the network, for example, using tools like OpenSSL or GnuPG to encrypt sensitive data stored on a mobile device or transmitted over the internet, inadequate encryption can expose users to data breaches, identity theft, or unauthorized access to confidential information, insecure app permissions are a significant risk for mobile devices, as many apps request excessive permissions that grant access to sensitive device resources or personal information, for example, using tools like apktool or jadx to decompile and analyze Android apps for suspicious or excessive permissions, insecure app permissions can lead to data leakage, privacy violations, or unauthorized access to device resources, lack of patch management and software updates are significant risks for mobile devices, as many users fail to update their devices with the latest security patches and software updates, for example, using tools like Google Play Protect or Samsung Knox to scan for and install security updates on Android devices, lack of patch management and software updates can leave devices vulnerable to known security vulnerabilities and exploits, exposing users to malware infections, data breaches, or other security incidents, insecure device configurations are another common risk associated with mobile devices, as many users fail to configure their devices with appropriate security settings or disable unnecessary features or services, for example, using tools like Android

Debug Bridge (ADB) or Mobile Device Management (MDM) solutions to enforce security policies and configurations on mobile devices, insecure device configurations can expose users to security risks, such as unauthorized access, data breaches, or malware infections, lost or stolen devices are significant risks for mobile users, as lost or stolen devices can be easily accessed by unauthorized parties, for example, using tools like Find My iPhone or Android Device Manager to locate, lock, or wipe lost or stolen devices remotely, lost or stolen devices can result in data loss, identity theft, or unauthorized access to sensitive information, securing mobile devices requires a multi-layered approach that addresses the various risks and vulnerabilities associated with mobile technology, for example, implementing strong authentication, encryption, access controls, and device management solutions to protect mobile devices and data, organizations should also educate users about mobile security best practices, such as avoiding insecure Wi-Fi networks, keeping devices up-to-date with security patches and software updates, and using strong passwords or biometric authentication methods to protect device access, proactive monitoring and incident response are essential for detecting and responding to mobile security incidents, for example, using tools like Mobile Threat Defense (MTD) solutions or Security Information and Event Management (SIEM) systems to monitor mobile device activity and alert on suspicious or malicious behavior, proactive monitoring and incident response can help organizations mitigate the impact of mobile security incidents and prevent data breaches or other security incidents. Mobile application security testing approaches are crucial for ensuring the integrity and reliability of mobile applications, given the widespread use of mobile devices and the sensitive data they often handle, one common approach to mobile application security testing is static analysis, which involves examining the application's source code or binary code without executing it, for example, using tools like MobSF (Mobile Security Framework) or QARK (Quick Android Review Kit) to analyze Android application packages (APKs) for security vulnerabilities and coding errors, static analysis helps identify potential security vulnerabilities, such as insecure data storage, hardcoded credentials, or improper input validation, another approach is dynamic analysis, which involves executing the application in a controlled environment and observing its behavior to identify security vulnerabilities or weaknesses, for example, using tools like OWASP ZAP (Zed Attack Proxy) or Burp Suite to intercept and analyze HTTP(S) traffic generated by the mobile application during runtime, dynamic analysis helps identify runtime security vulnerabilities, such as insecure network communication, sensitive data leakage, or improper session management, a third approach is interactive testing, which involves manually testing the application's functionality and security features in real-time, for example, using tools like Frida or Appium to interact with the application's user interface (UI) and simulate user interactions, interactive testing helps identify user interface flaws, logical vulnerabilities, or authentication bypass vulnerabilities, a fourth approach is binary analysis, which involves examining the application's binary code to identify security vulnerabilities or weaknesses, for example, using tools like IDA Pro or Ghidra to disassemble and analyze the application's binary code for potential security vulnerabilities, binary analysis helps identify low-level security vulnerabilities, such as buffer overflows, code injection, or memory corruption, a fifth approach is fuzz testing, which involves sending invalid, unexpected, or random data to the application's input fields to identify potential security vulnerabilities or crashes, for example, using tools like AFL (American Fuzzy Lop) or Peach Fuzzer to generate and send fuzzed input to the application and monitor its behavior, fuzz testing helps identify input validation flaws, buffer overflows, or other security vulnerabilities that could be exploited by attackers, a sixth approach is reverse engineering, which involves decompiling or disassembling the application's binary code to understand its internal workings and identify potential security vulnerabilities, for example, using tools like JADX or Hopper to decompile and analyze the application's bytecode or machine code, reverse engineering helps identify hidden functionality, obfuscated code, or security vulnerabilities that are not easily discoverable through other testing approaches, a seventh approach is penetration testing, which involves simulating real-world attacks on the application to identify security vulnerabilities or weaknesses, for example, using tools like Metasploit or OWASP Mobile Security Testing Guide to perform penetration tests on the application and assess its security posture, penetration testing helps identify exploitable security vulnerabilities, such as authentication bypass, SQL injection, or remote code execution, a eighth approach is behavioral analysis, which involves monitoring the application's runtime behavior to identify suspicious or malicious activity, for example, using tools like Sysdig or strace to monitor system calls and network activity generated by the application during runtime, behavioral analysis helps identify anomalous behavior, malware infections, or security incidents that may indicate a security vulnerability or compromise, a ninth approach is compliance testing, which involves assessing the application's compliance with industry standards, regulations, or security best practices, for example, using tools like OWASP Mobile Top 10 or NIST Mobile Application Security Testing (MAST) to evaluate the application against relevant security standards and guidelines, compliance testing helps identify security weaknesses or gaps in the application's implementation or design, a tenth approach is continuous integration and continuous deployment (CI/CD) testing, which involves integrating security testing into the software development lifecycle (SDLC) to identify and remediate security vulnerabilities early in the development process, for example, using tools like Jenkins or GitLab CI/CD to automate security testing tasks, such as static analysis, dynamic analysis, or code review, CI/CD testing helps ensure that security vulnerabilities are addressed promptly and efficiently, improving the overall security posture of the application, selecting the appropriate testing approach depends on various factors, including the application's complexity, development stage, target platform, and security requirements, organizations should adopt a comprehensive testing strategy that combines multiple testing approaches to maximize coverage and effectiveness in identifying and mitigating security vulnerabilities in mobile applications.

Chapter 9: Cloud Security Vulnerability Analysis

Cloud computing security considerations are paramount in today's digital landscape, given the widespread adoption of cloud services and the increasing reliance on cloud infrastructure for storing, processing, and managing data, one key consideration is data security, as organizations entrust cloud service providers (CSPs) with sensitive data, such as customer information, financial records, or intellectual property, ensuring the confidentiality, integrity, and availability of data stored in the cloud is essential, for example, using encryption techniques such as AES (Advanced Encryption Standard) or RSA (Rivest-Shamir-Adleman) to encrypt data before storing it in the cloud and managing encryption keys securely, data security measures also include access controls, authentication mechanisms, and audit trails to prevent unauthorized access, data breaches, or data loss, another consideration is compliance and regulatory requirements, as organizations must comply with various industry regulations, such as GDPR (General Data Protection Regulation), HIPAA (Health Insurance Portability and Accountability Act), or PCI DSS (Payment Card Industry Data Security Standard), ensuring that cloud services comply with relevant regulations and standards is crucial for avoiding legal penalties, fines, or reputational damage, for example, using cloud service providers that offer compliance certifications or attestations, such as SOC 2 (Service Organization Control 2) or ISO 27001 (International Organization for Standardization), to demonstrate adherence to industry best practices and regulatory requirements, third-party risk management is another critical consideration in cloud computing security, as organizations rely on cloud service providers to deliver reliable and secure services, assessing the security posture of cloud service providers and evaluating their capabilities, processes, and controls is essential for mitigating third-party risks, for example, conducting security assessments, audits, or due diligence reviews of cloud service providers to evaluate their security practices, incident response capabilities, and data protection measures, network security is also a significant consideration in cloud computing, as data traverses networks and internet connections to access cloud services and resources, securing network connections, implementing firewalls, intrusion detection systems (IDS), and intrusion prevention systems (IPS), and using virtual private networks (VPN) or secure tunnels to encrypt network traffic are essential for protecting data in transit, for example, configuring network security groups (NSGs) or security groups (SGs) to control inbound and outbound traffic to cloud resources and applying access control lists (ACLs) or security policies to restrict network access, identity and access management (IAM) is another critical consideration in cloud computing security, as organizations must manage user identities, permissions, and privileges to prevent unauthorized access or misuse of cloud resources, implementing strong authentication mechanisms, multi-factor authentication (MFA), and role-based access control (RBAC) policies to enforce the principle of least privilege and limit access to sensitive data and resources, for example, using identity providers (IdPs) such as Azure Active Directory (AAD) or AWS Identity and Access Management (IAM) to authenticate and authorize users, enforcing strong password policies, and periodically reviewing and revoking access permissions, security incident detection and response is essential for detecting and responding to security incidents and breaches in cloud environments, implementing security monitoring, logging, and alerting mechanisms to detect anomalous activities, unauthorized access attempts, or suspicious behavior, and establishing incident response processes, procedures, and protocols to investigate security incidents, mitigate their impact, and restore normal operations, for example, using cloud-native security tools, such as AWS CloudTrail, Azure Security Center, or Google Cloud Security Command Center (Cloud SCC), to monitor and analyze cloud activity, generate audit logs, and alert on security events, continuous security monitoring, and auditing are crucial for maintaining the security posture of cloud environments, implementing automated security monitoring, vulnerability scanning, and configuration management tools to identify security risks, misconfigurations, or vulnerabilities in cloud infrastructure, applications, or data, and performing regular security assessments, audits, or penetration tests to validate security controls, identify weaknesses, and address security gaps, for example, using cloud security posture management (CSPM) tools, such as Palo Alto Networks Prisma Cloud or Trend Micro Cloud One Conformity, to continuously monitor cloud configurations, assess compliance with security best practices, and remediate security issues, educating users and stakeholders about cloud computing security risks, best practices, and responsibilities is essential for building a security-aware culture and promoting cybersecurity awareness, providing security training, awareness programs, and resources to employees, customers, partners, and vendors to educate them about common security threats, phishing attacks, data protection practices, and security hygiene, and encouraging proactive reporting of security incidents, suspicious activities, or potential vulnerabilities to the appropriate security teams or authorities, fostering collaboration and information sharing among stakeholders, industry peers, and cybersecurity communities is essential for addressing emerging security threats, sharing threat intelligence, and leveraging collective expertise and resources to enhance cloud computing security, participating in industry forums, information sharing organizations, or threat intelligence platforms to exchange security insights, best practices, and threat intelligence, and collaborating with cloud service providers, security vendors, government agencies, and regulatory bodies to address shared security challenges, develop security standards, and promote cybersecurity awareness and resilience, embracing a risk-based approach to cloud computing security is essential for identifying, assessing, and prioritizing security risks, vulnerabilities, and threats, aligning security controls and investments with business objectives, regulatory requirements, and risk tolerance levels, and making informed decisions about risk mitigation strategies, controls, and investments, for example, conducting risk assessments, threat modeling, or security risk analysis to identify and prioritize security risks, assess their potential impact, and develop risk mitigation plans, integrating security into the cloud computing lifecycle is essential for ensuring that security considerations are addressed at every stage of the cloud adoption journey, integrating security requirements, controls, and processes into cloud architecture, design, development, deployment, and operations, and adopting secure coding practices, DevSecOps principles, and security automation to build, deploy, and manage secure cloud applications and services, for example, incorporating security requirements into cloud architecture frameworks, such as AWS Well-Architected Framework or Microsoft Azure Security Benchmarks, and integrating security testing, code analysis, and vulnerability management tools into CI/CD pipelines, monitoring and adapting to evolving threats, technologies, and regulatory requirements is essential for maintaining the effectiveness and resilience of cloud computing security controls, monitoring emerging security threats, vulnerabilities, and attack techniques, and leveraging threat intelligence, security advisories, and industry insights to update security controls, policies, and procedures, for example, subscribing to security alerts, bulletins, or advisories from cloud service providers, security vendors, or government agencies, and conducting regular security reviews, assessments, or audits to evaluate the effectiveness of security controls, identify areas for improvement, and ensure compliance with security policies and standards. Cloud penetration testing and risk assessment are crucial components of ensuring the security and resilience of cloud environments, as organizations increasingly rely on cloud services and infrastructure to store, process, and manage their data and applications, conducting penetration tests helps identify security vulnerabilities, weaknesses, and misconfigurations in cloud infrastructure, applications, and services that could be exploited by attackers, penetration testing simulates real-world cyber attacks to assess the effectiveness of security controls, policies, and procedures in detecting, preventing, and mitigating security threats, for example, using penetration testing frameworks such as Metasploit or Burp Suite to perform reconnaissance, vulnerability scanning, and exploitation of cloud resources and applications, penetration testing methodologies typically include reconnaissance, information gathering, vulnerability analysis, exploitation, post-exploitation, and reporting phases, for example, using tools like Nmap or Shodan to discover and enumerate cloud assets, services, and vulnerabilities, and using automated vulnerability scanning tools like Nessus or OpenVAS to identify security weaknesses, misconfigurations, or outdated software versions, conducting manual security testing, code review, or configuration review of cloud infrastructure, applications, and APIs to identify security vulnerabilities, logic flaws, or authentication bypass vulnerabilities, for example, using static analysis tools like SonarQube or Checkmarx to analyze source code for security vulnerabilities, or using dynamic analysis tools like OWASP ZAP or Burp Suite to intercept and manipulate HTTP(S) requests and responses, identifying common security vulnerabilities, such as injection flaws, broken authentication, insecure direct object references, security misconfigurations, or sensitive data exposure, and exploiting security vulnerabilities to gain unauthorized access, escalate privileges, or exfiltrate sensitive data from cloud environments, for example, using SQL injection, cross-site scripting (XSS), or XML external entity (XXE) attacks to exploit vulnerabilities in web applications running on cloud platforms, or using misconfigured permissions, weak passwords, or insecure network configurations to compromise cloud infrastructure or services, conducting post-exploitation activities, such as lateral movement, privilege escalation, or data exfiltration, to assess the impact of a successful attack and identify additional security weaknesses or attack vectors, for example, using tools like BloodHound or CrackMapExec to map network topology, identify privileged accounts, and exploit trust relationships between systems in a cloud environment, or using data exfiltration techniques like steganography or covert channels to exfiltrate sensitive information from compromised cloud instances, documenting and reporting security findings, including identified vulnerabilities, exploited weaknesses, attack paths, and recommendations for remediation, for example, using penetration testing reports, executive summaries, or risk matrices to communicate security risks, prioritize remediation efforts, and guide security improvements, conducting cloud risk assessments helps organizations identify, analyze, and prioritize security risks and threats to their cloud environments, applications, and data, risk assessments help organizations understand the likelihood and potential impact of security threats, vulnerabilities, and incidents on their cloud assets, for example, using risk assessment frameworks like NIST SP 800-30 or ISO/IEC 27005 to assess and quantify security risks in cloud environments, conducting threat modeling exercises to identify and prioritize potential threats, attack vectors, and security controls, for example, using tools like Microsoft Threat Modeling Tool or OWASP Threat Dragon to model threats, vulnerabilities, and security controls in cloud applications and services, analyzing security controls, policies, and procedures to identify gaps, weaknesses, or deficiencies in cloud security posture, for example, reviewing cloud security configurations, access controls, encryption mechanisms, logging and monitoring practices, incident response procedures, and disaster recovery plans, identifying dependencies, interdependencies, and relationships between cloud assets, services, and stakeholders to understand the potential impact of security incidents on business operations, for example, mapping cloud service dependencies, data flows, and critical business processes to identify single points of failure, data bottlenecks, or regulatory compliance requirements, evaluating the effectiveness of existing security controls and countermeasures in mitigating identified risks and threats, for example, assessing the effectiveness of access controls, authentication mechanisms, encryption algorithms, intrusion detection and prevention systems (IDS/IPS), and security monitoring tools in detecting, preventing, or mitigating security incidents, documenting and communicating risk assessment findings, including identified risks, recommended risk treatment options, and risk acceptance decisions, for example, using risk assessment reports, risk registers, or risk matrices to document and communicate security risks, vulnerabilities, and treatment plans to stakeholders, including senior management, business owners, and technical teams, integrating risk assessment into the cloud governance and risk management processes to ensure that security risks are identified, assessed, and managed effectively throughout the cloud lifecycle, for example, incorporating risk assessment into cloud procurement, deployment, operations, and decommissioning processes, and reviewing and updating risk assessments regularly to address changes in cloud environments, technologies, threats, or business requirements, for example, conducting periodic risk assessments, security audits, or compliance reviews to reassess security risks, update risk treatment plans, and ensure ongoing compliance with security policies, standards, and regulations.

Chapter 10: Advanced Vulnerability Research and Exploitation

Zero-day vulnerability research is a critical aspect of cybersecurity that focuses on identifying and analyzing previously unknown security vulnerabilities in software, hardware, or firmware, zero-day vulnerabilities, also known as 0-days, are vulnerabilities that are exploited by attackers before the software vendor or developer becomes aware of them, conducting zero-day vulnerability research involves a combination of reverse engineering, code analysis, fuzzing, and exploit development techniques to discover and exploit security weaknesses, reverse engineering is the process of analyzing software binaries, firmware, or hardware components to understand their functionality, structure, and behavior, for example, using disassemblers, decompilers, or debuggers to reverse engineer executable code, analyzing software binaries or firmware images to identify vulnerabilities, or extract sensitive information, code analysis involves reviewing source code, binaries, or firmware images to identify security vulnerabilities, coding errors, or logic flaws that could be exploited by attackers, for example, using static code analysis tools like

IDA Pro, Ghidra, or Binary Ninja to analyze executable code, identify function calls, control flow paths, or data structures, or using dynamic code analysis tools like debuggers or memory profilers to analyze runtime behavior, memory usage, or resource consumption, fuzzing is a technique used to discover vulnerabilities by sending malformed or unexpected inputs to software applications, protocols, or file formats and observing their behavior, for example, using fuzzing frameworks like AFL (American Fuzzy Lop), Peach Fuzzer, or Radamsa to generate and send input mutations to target software, protocols, or file formats, and monitoring for crashes, hangs, or unexpected behavior, exploit development involves creating proof-of-concept (PoC) exploits or weaponized exploits to demonstrate the impact of a vulnerability and exploit it for malicious purposes, for example, using scripting languages like Python or Ruby to develop exploit code, crafting payloads, shellcode, or exploit chains to trigger buffer overflows, code execution, or privilege escalation, conducting zero-day vulnerability research requires a deep understanding of computer systems, software architecture, programming languages, and security principles, as well as proficiency in various tools, techniques, and methodologies used in vulnerability discovery and exploitation, for example, understanding memory corruption vulnerabilities like buffer overflows, integer overflows, or format string vulnerabilities, and how they can be exploited to gain unauthorized access or execute arbitrary code, knowledge of network protocols, file formats, or cryptographic algorithms and how they can be manipulated or abused to bypass security controls or compromise systems, familiarity with security testing frameworks, fuzzing techniques, or exploit development platforms, and proficiency in using debugging tools, disassemblers, or code analysis utilities to analyze, understand, and manipulate software binaries, conducting zero-day vulnerability research requires a methodical and systematic approach to identify, analyze, and exploit security vulnerabilities, starting with reconnaissance and information gathering to identify potential targets, attack surfaces, or entry points, for example, using tools like Shodan, Nmap, or Censys to discover internet-facing systems, services, or devices, identifying potential attack vectors, attack surfaces, or entry points, or using vulnerability intelligence feeds, security advisories, or exploit databases to identify known vulnerabilities in target software, conducting vulnerability analysis and assessment to identify security weaknesses, coding errors, or logic flaws that could be exploited by attackers, for example, using static and dynamic code analysis techniques to review source code, binaries, or firmware images for common security vulnerabilities, such as buffer overflows, input validation errors, or insecure cryptographic implementations, or using manual code review techniques to identify logic flaws, race conditions, or privilege escalation vulnerabilities, developing proof-of-concept (PoC) exploits or weaponized exploits to demonstrate the impact of a vulnerability and exploit it for malicious purposes, for example, crafting exploit payloads, shellcode, or exploit chains to trigger buffer overflows, code execution, or privilege escalation, and testing and validating the exploit to ensure that it works reliably and as intended, for example, testing the exploit against different target platforms, configurations, or versions to verify its effectiveness and reliability, documenting and reporting the vulnerability research findings, including identified vulnerabilities, exploited weaknesses, attack vectors, and recommendations for remediation, for example, documenting the steps taken to identify, analyze, and exploit the vulnerability, including the tools, techniques, and methodologies used, and providing detailed recommendations for mitigating the security risks and addressing the root causes of the vulnerabilities, sharing the vulnerability research findings with relevant stakeholders, including software vendors, developers, security researchers, or industry groups, for example, submitting vulnerability reports to bug bounty programs, security advisories, or coordination centers, and collaborating with vendors, developers, or security communities to develop and deploy patches, updates, or mitigations, conducting ongoing research and monitoring to stay abreast of emerging threats, vulnerabilities, and attack techniques, for example, monitoring security mailing lists, forums, or social media channels for discussions, disclosures, or reports of zero-day vulnerabilities, and participating in security conferences, workshops, or training events to exchange knowledge, share insights, and learn about new tools and techniques. Advanced exploitation techniques and defense strategies are crucial aspects of cybersecurity that focus on both offensive and defensive tactics to protect systems and networks from sophisticated attacks, advanced exploitation techniques involve leveraging complex vulnerabilities, exploiting weaknesses in software, hardware, or network protocols, and bypassing security controls to gain unauthorized access, execute arbitrary code, or escalate privileges, while defense strategies focus on implementing robust security measures, detecting and mitigating security threats, and improving overall security posture, advanced exploitation techniques often involve the use of sophisticated tools, techniques, and methodologies to identify, exploit, and manipulate security vulnerabilities, for example, using memory corruption exploits like buffer overflows, heap overflows, or use-after-free vulnerabilities to execute arbitrary code, achieve remote code execution, or bypass exploit mitigations, or using logic flaws, race conditions, or side-channel attacks to bypass authentication mechanisms, escalate privileges, or gain unauthorized access, defense strategies involve implementing multiple layers of security controls, including preventive, detective, and corrective measures, to defend against advanced exploitation techniques and mitigate security risks, for example, deploying intrusion detection and prevention systems (IDS/IPS), firewalls, antivirus software, and endpoint protection solutions to detect and block malicious activities, conducting vulnerability assessments, penetration tests, and code reviews to identify and remediate security vulnerabilities before they can be exploited by attackers, or using secure coding practices, input validation, and error handling to prevent common security vulnerabilities, such as buffer overflows, injection flaws, or authentication bypass vulnerabilities, advanced exploitation techniques often target specific software applications, operating systems, or hardware platforms, and may require in-depth knowledge of software architecture, memory management, and CPU internals, for example, using stack-based buffer overflows to overwrite return addresses, hijack control flow, or execute arbitrary code in the context of a vulnerable process, or using heap-based exploitation techniques to corrupt heap data structures, manipulate memory allocations, or achieve code execution, defense strategies involve implementing security best practices, security controls, and security policies to protect systems and networks from exploitation, for example, applying security updates, patches, and hotfixes to address known vulnerabilities, vulnerabilities, or using virtual patching, intrusion detection, or network segmentation to mitigate the risk of exploitation, deploying endpoint protection solutions, application whitelisting, or containerization to prevent malicious code execution, privilege escalation, or lateral movement, or using threat intelligence feeds, security information and event management (SIEM) solutions, or security analytics platforms to detect and respond to security threats in real-time, advanced exploitation techniques often require advanced knowledge of operating system internals, network protocols, and software vulnerabilities, and may involve the use of custom-developed exploit code or publicly available exploit kits, for example, using advanced debugging techniques, reverse engineering tools, or kernel-mode exploits to bypass security mechanisms, exploit zero-day vulnerabilities, or escalate privileges, defense strategies involve implementing defense-in-depth strategies, security controls, and security measures to protect against known and unknown threats, for example, using network segmentation, least privilege, or role-based access controls (RBAC) to limit the impact of successful attacks, conducting security awareness training, security audits, or security assessments to educate users, raise awareness about security risks, and improve security hygiene, or using incident response plans, disaster recovery plans, or business continuity plans to minimize the impact of security incidents, recover from security breaches, and maintain business operations, advanced exploitation techniques and defense strategies are constantly evolving in response to emerging threats, vulnerabilities, and attack techniques, and require ongoing research, training, and collaboration between security professionals, researchers, and industry stakeholders to stay ahead of adversaries, for example, participating in bug bounty programs, security conferences, or capture the flag (CTF) competitions to learn about new exploit techniques, vulnerability research, and defensive strategies, or collaborating with vendors, developers, or security communities to share threat intelligence, security best practices, and mitigation techniques.

BOOK 3
THREAT INTELLIGENCE FUNDAMENTALS
ADVANCED STRATEGIES FOR CYSA+ EXAM CS0-003

ROB BOTWRIGHT

Chapter 1: Introduction to Threat Intelligence

The significance of threat intelligence cannot be overstated in the realm of cybersecurity, it serves as a cornerstone in the proactive defense against evolving cyber threats, threat intelligence encompasses the collection, analysis, and dissemination of information about potential and ongoing cyber threats, it provides organizations with valuable insights into the tactics, techniques, and procedures (TTPs) employed by threat actors, enabling them to anticipate, detect, and respond to attacks more effectively, leveraging threat intelligence allows organizations to make informed decisions about their cybersecurity posture, resource allocation, and risk mitigation strategies, by understanding the motives, capabilities, and behaviors of threat actors, organizations can prioritize their security efforts and allocate resources more efficiently, threat intelligence sources include open-source intelligence (OSINT), dark web monitoring, information sharing platforms, security vendors, government agencies, and industry-specific information sharing and analysis centers (ISACs), OSINT refers to publicly available information from websites, social media platforms, forums, blogs, and other online sources, it provides valuable insights into emerging threats, vulnerabilities, and attack techniques, dark web monitoring involves monitoring underground forums, marketplaces, and chat rooms on the dark web for discussions, advertisements, and sales related to cybercrime, information sharing platforms facilitate the exchange of threat intelligence between organizations, security vendors, and government agencies, they enable organizations to collaborate, share insights, and leverage collective knowledge to enhance their security posture, threat intelligence analysis involves processing, correlating, and contextualizing raw data to identify patterns, trends, and anomalies indicative of potential threats, it requires specialized tools, techniques, and expertise to analyze large volumes of data from diverse sources and extract actionable intelligence, threat intelligence platforms (TIPs) are software solutions that facilitate the collection, enrichment, analysis, and dissemination of threat intelligence, they enable organizations to centralize their threat intelligence operations, automate workflows, and integrate with existing security tools and processes, TIPs provide features such as data ingestion, normalization, enrichment, correlation, visualization, and reporting, they enable analysts to aggregate threat data from multiple sources, enrich it with contextual information, and prioritize it based on relevance and severity, deploying a threat intelligence platform involves several steps, including requirements gathering, vendor evaluation, solution design, implementation, integration, and training, organizations should assess their specific needs, objectives, and budget constraints before selecting a TIP vendor, they should evaluate factors such as data sources, data formats, scalability, performance, usability, and support, once a TIP has been selected, organizations should define their use cases, workflows, and processes for ingesting, analyzing, and acting on threat intelligence, they should integrate the TIP with existing security tools and processes, such as security information and event management (SIEM) systems, intrusion detection systems (IDS), and security orchestration, automation, and response (SOAR) platforms, organizations should also establish policies and procedures for sharing threat intelligence with trusted partners, industry peers, and relevant authorities, threat intelligence enables organizations to enhance their situational awareness, detect early indicators of compromise (IOCs), and respond to security incidents more effectively, it empowers security teams to identify emerging threats, vulnerabilities, and attack trends, enabling them to adapt their defenses and mitigate risks proactively, threat intelligence also enables organizations to improve their incident response capabilities, by providing real-time insights into ongoing attacks, it helps organizations prioritize and coordinate their response efforts, allocate resources, and contain the impact of security incidents, threat intelligence is an essential component of a comprehensive cybersecurity strategy, it enables organizations to stay ahead of adversaries, anticipate their moves, and defend against evolving threats effectively, organizations that leverage threat intelligence can better protect their assets, data, and reputation in an increasingly complex and dynamic threat landscape. Components of threat intelligence programs encompass various elements essential for effective cybersecurity defense strategies, understanding these components is critical for organizations aiming to establish robust threat intelligence capabilities, the first component involves defining the objectives and scope of the threat intelligence program, organizations must identify their specific goals, such as improving threat detection, enhancing incident response, or reducing the organization's overall risk exposure, defining the scope involves determining the types of threats, adversaries, and assets that the program will focus on, whether it's targeting specific industries, regions, or types of attacks, once the objectives and scope are established, the next component is data collection, this involves gathering information from internal and external sources, including open-source intelligence (OSINT), dark web monitoring, threat feeds, security vendors, government agencies, and industry-specific information sharing and analysis centers (ISACs), organizations should collect a diverse range of data types, such as indicators of compromise (IOCs), threat actor profiles, malware samples, vulnerability data, and security advisories, the collected data must be processed and analyzed to extract actionable intelligence, which brings us to the third component, data analysis and enrichment, this involves analyzing the raw data to identify patterns, trends, and anomalies indicative of potential threats, enriching the data involves adding contextual information, such as threat actor profiles, attack techniques, and mitigation strategies, to enhance its relevance and usefulness, data analysis and enrichment require specialized tools, techniques, and expertise to correlate and contextualize large volumes of data from diverse sources, once the data is analyzed and enriched, it must be disseminated to the appropriate stakeholders, which brings us to the fourth component, information sharing and dissemination, organizations should share threat intelligence with internal teams, such as security operations, incident response, and threat hunting teams, as well as external partners, such as industry peers, trusted vendors, and relevant authorities, information sharing enables organizations to collaborate, coordinate, and respond to threats more effectively, it helps to build a collective defense against cyber threats and improve overall security posture, the fifth component is threat intelligence integration, this involves integrating threat intelligence into existing security tools and processes, such as security information and event management (SIEM) systems, intrusion detection systems (IDS), security orchestration, automation, and response (SOAR) platforms, and endpoint detection and response (EDR) solutions, integration enables organizations to automate threat detection, investigation, and response, reducing the time to detect and mitigate security incidents, it also allows organizations to correlate threat intelligence with security events, alerts, and incidents, providing context and prioritization, finally, the sixth component is continuous improvement and evaluation, threat intelligence programs must be continuously evaluated and refined to ensure their effectiveness and relevance, this involves monitoring key performance indicators (KPIs), such as the number of threats detected, the time to respond to incidents, and the impact of security measures, organizations should regularly review their objectives, processes, and tools, and make adjustments based on lessons learned, emerging threats, and changing business requirements, by continuously improving their threat intelligence capabilities, organizations can stay ahead of adversaries and better protect their assets, data, and reputation in an increasingly complex and dynamic threat landscape.

Chapter 2: Cyber Threat Landscape Analysis

Analyzing current cyber threat trends is paramount for organizations to stay abreast of the ever-evolving landscape of cybersecurity risks, understanding these trends provides valuable insights into the tactics, techniques, and procedures (TTPs) employed by threat actors, enabling organizations to fortify their defenses and mitigate potential risks effectively, one prevalent cyber threat trend is the rise of ransomware attacks, ransomware has become increasingly sophisticated and pervasive, targeting organizations of all sizes and industries, attackers exploit vulnerabilities in software, networks, and human behavior to infiltrate systems and encrypt critical data, demanding ransom payments in exchange for decryption keys, another significant trend is the proliferation of phishing attacks, phishing remains one of the most common and effective methods used by cybercriminals to compromise organizations, attackers craft convincing emails, messages, or websites to trick users into revealing sensitive information, downloading malicious attachments, or clicking on malicious links, resulting in data breaches, financial losses, and reputational damage, additionally, supply chain attacks have emerged as a growing concern for organizations, attackers target third-party vendors, suppliers, or service providers to gain unauthorized access to their networks and infiltrate their customers' systems, supply chain attacks can have far-reaching consequences, impacting multiple organizations and compromising the integrity of products, services, or data, moreover, there has been a surge in attacks targeting remote workers and home networks, with the widespread adoption of remote work due to the COVID-19 pandemic, attackers have shifted their focus to exploiting vulnerabilities in remote access technologies, virtual private networks (VPNs), and collaboration tools, posing significant security risks for organizations with remote workforce, furthermore, nation-state actors continue to pose a significant threat to organizations and critical infrastructure, state-sponsored cyber espionage, sabotage, and disinformation campaigns have escalated in recent years, targeting governments, businesses, and other entities for political, economic, or strategic purposes, organizations must also contend with emerging threats such as zero-day exploits, fileless malware, and attacks targeting internet of things (IoT) devices, these threats leverage novel techniques and exploit previously unknown vulnerabilities, making them difficult to detect and mitigate, analyzing current cyber threat trends requires a multifaceted approach, organizations should monitor threat intelligence feeds, security blogs, research reports, and industry publications for insights into emerging threats and attack techniques, they should also leverage threat intelligence platforms (TIPs) and security information and event management (SIEM) systems to aggregate, correlate, and analyze security data from diverse sources, identifying patterns, anomalies, and indicators of compromise (IOCs), organizations should conduct regular risk assessments and security audits to identify vulnerabilities, gaps, and weaknesses in their security posture, and prioritize remediation efforts accordingly, implementing layered security controls, such as firewalls, intrusion detection and prevention systems (IDS/IPS), endpoint protection solutions, and security awareness training, can help organizations defend against a wide range of cyber threats, organizations should also establish incident response plans, playbooks, and procedures to ensure a timely and coordinated response to security incidents, minimizing the impact and disruption caused by cyber attacks, by staying vigilant, informed, and proactive, organizations can better protect themselves against the evolving threatscape and safeguard their assets, data, and reputation from cyber threats. Emerging threats pose significant challenges to cybersecurity professionals, as they constantly evolve and adapt to exploit vulnerabilities in systems, networks, and applications, understanding these threats and their potential impact is crucial for organizations to effectively mitigate risks and protect their assets, one emerging threat is the proliferation of Internet of Things (IoT) devices, IoT devices, such as smart thermostats, security cameras, and wearable devices, are increasingly being connected to corporate networks, creating new avenues for cyber attacks, attackers can exploit vulnerabilities in IoT devices to gain unauthorized access to networks, launch distributed denial-of-service (DDoS) attacks, or steal sensitive data, another emerging threat is the rise of artificial intelligence (AI) and machine learning (ML) powered attacks, attackers are leveraging AI and ML algorithms to automate and enhance various aspects of cyber attacks, including reconnaissance, evasion, and decision-making, making them more sophisticated and difficult to detect, moreover, supply chain attacks have emerged as a growing concern for organizations, attackers target third-party vendors, suppliers, or service providers to gain unauthorized access to their networks and infiltrate their customers' systems, supply chain attacks can have far-reaching consequences, impacting multiple organizations and compromising the integrity of products, services, or data, additionally, ransomware attacks continue to evolve in sophistication and scale, with attackers using advanced techniques such as double extortion and data exfiltration to maximize their profits and coerce victims into paying ransoms, ransomware attacks can disrupt operations, cause financial losses, and damage reputation, furthermore, attacks targeting cloud infrastructure and services are on the rise, as organizations increasingly migrate their workloads and data to the cloud, attackers are exploiting misconfigurations, weak credentials, and vulnerabilities in cloud environments to gain unauthorized access, steal data, or disrupt services, organizations must also contend with the growing threat of insider threats, malicious insiders, whether employees, contractors, or partners, can pose a significant risk to organizations by abusing their privileges, stealing sensitive data, or sabotaging systems, insider threats can be difficult to detect and mitigate, as insiders often have legitimate access to sensitive systems and information, analyzing emerging threats and their impact requires organizations to adopt a proactive and multi-layered approach to cybersecurity, organizations should continuously monitor their networks, systems, and applications for signs of suspicious activity, leveraging tools such as intrusion detection systems (IDS), intrusion prevention systems (IPS), and security information and event management (SIEM) solutions, they should also conduct regular security assessments and penetration testing to identify and remediate vulnerabilities, educate employees about the risks of emerging threats and how to recognize and report suspicious activity, implementing strong access controls, least privilege principles, and multi-factor authentication (MFA) can help organizations mitigate the risk of insider threats, organizations should also establish incident response plans, playbooks, and procedures to ensure a timely and coordinated response to security incidents, minimizing the impact and disruption caused by cyber attacks, by staying informed, vigilant, and proactive, organizations can better protect themselves against emerging threats and safeguard their assets, data, and reputation from cyber attacks.

Chapter 3: Threat Actor Profiling and Attribution

Understanding threat actor motivations is essential for cybersecurity professionals to develop effective defense strategies and mitigate risks effectively, threat actors, whether individuals, groups, or nation-states, have diverse motivations driving their malicious activities, one common motivation is financial gain, cybercriminals engage in various activities such as ransomware attacks, phishing scams, and credit card fraud to steal money or valuable assets, another motivation is ideological or political beliefs, hacktivists and cyber terrorists target organizations, governments, or individuals to promote their agendas, spread propaganda, or disrupt operations, moreover, espionage is another common motivation for threat actors, nation-states and state-sponsored groups conduct cyber espionage to steal sensitive information, intellectual property, or government secrets for strategic, economic, or political advantage, additionally, some threat actors engage in sabotage or vandalism, disrupting operations, destroying data, or causing physical damage to systems or infrastructure, this may be motivated by revenge, retaliation, or a desire to undermine competitors or adversaries, furthermore, insider threats represent a significant concern for organizations, employees, contractors, or partners with legitimate access to systems and information may abuse their privileges for personal gain, sabotage, or espionage, understanding the motivations behind insider threats can help organizations detect and mitigate risks more effectively, understanding threat actor motivations requires gathering intelligence and analyzing their behavior, organizations can use various sources of threat intelligence, including open-source intelligence (OSINT), dark web monitoring, and intelligence sharing partnerships, to gain insights into threat actor motivations, behavior, and tactics, techniques, and procedures (TTPs), they can also conduct threat modeling exercises to identify potential threats and assess their likelihood and impact, furthermore, organizations can use behavioral analytics and machine learning algorithms to detect anomalous behavior indicative of malicious activity, identifying patterns and trends in cyber attacks can help organizations anticipate and prepare for future threats, organizations should also consider the geopolitical and socio-economic factors that influence threat actor motivations, such as regional conflicts, economic downturns, or political tensions, understanding the broader context can provide valuable insights into the motives and intentions of threat actors, enabling organizations to better anticipate and respond to emerging threats, finally, collaboration and information sharing among organizations, government agencies, and law enforcement can help identify and disrupt cybercriminal activities, sharing threat intelligence, best practices, and lessons learned can enhance collective defense and resilience against cyber threats, by understanding threat actor motivations and behavior, organizations can better protect themselves against cyber attacks and mitigate the impact of security incidents on their operations, reputation, and bottom line. Techniques for attribution and profiling play a crucial role in cybersecurity investigations, attribution refers to identifying the individuals, groups, or organizations behind cyber attacks, while profiling involves gathering information about their characteristics, motives, and capabilities, attribution is often challenging due to the anonymity and obfuscation techniques used by threat actors to conceal their identities and origins, however, several techniques can help investigators trace attacks back to their source, one common technique is analyzing indicators of compromise (IOCs), IOCs are artifacts or evidence left behind by attackers during their operations, such as IP addresses, domain names, file hashes, or malware signatures, organizations can use security tools such as intrusion detection systems (IDS) or endpoint detection and response (EDR) solutions to collect and analyze IOCs from their networks, enabling them to identify patterns and correlations indicative of specific threat actors or campaigns, another technique is conducting forensic analysis of compromised systems, forensic analysis involves collecting and analyzing digital evidence from computers, servers, or other electronic devices to reconstruct the timeline of events and identify the techniques used by attackers, investigators can use forensic tools such as EnCase or Autopsy to examine disk images, memory dumps, or network traffic logs for traces of malicious activity, moreover, threat intelligence sharing and collaboration can aid in attribution efforts, organizations can share IOCs, malware samples, and behavioral patterns with industry peers, government agencies, or cybersecurity researchers through information sharing platforms such as the Cyber Threat Intelligence Integration Center (CTIIC) or the Information Sharing and Analysis Centers (ISACs), facilitating collective analysis and attribution of cyber attacks, additionally, linguistic and behavioral analysis can provide insights into the characteristics and motivations of threat actors, linguists and psychologists analyze the language, syntax, and communication style used in threat actor communications, such as phishing emails, ransom notes, or online forums, to infer their nationality, cultural background, or psychological profile, furthermore, network traffic analysis can reveal valuable clues about the infrastructure and techniques used by threat actors, analysts can examine network logs, packet captures, or firewall logs to identify patterns of communication, command and control (C2) servers, or lateral movement within the network, enabling them to map out the infrastructure and infrastructure and tactics used by attackers, however, it is essential to exercise caution when attributing cyber attacks, as false attribution can have serious consequences, such as damaging diplomatic relations, escalating tensions, or provoking retaliatory actions, attribution should be based on multiple sources of evidence, corroborated by independent analysis and peer review, to ensure its accuracy and reliability, moreover, attribution efforts should be complemented by proactive defense measures, such as patching vulnerabilities, improving security awareness training, or deploying advanced threat detection capabilities, to mitigate the risk of future attacks, finally, legal and diplomatic considerations may also impact attribution efforts, particularly in cases involving nation-state actors or international cyber espionage, organizations should work closely with law enforcement agencies, government authorities, or diplomatic channels to coordinate attribution efforts and pursue appropriate responses or sanctions against threat actors, by employing a combination of technical, analytical, and collaborative techniques, organizations can enhance their ability to attribute cyber attacks accurately and effectively profile the perpetrators, enabling them to better defend against future threats and hold threat actors accountable for their actions.

Chapter 4: Open Source Intelligence (OSINT) Gathering

Leveraging open source data for threat intelligence is a valuable strategy for cybersecurity professionals to enhance their understanding of emerging threats and adversaries, open source data refers to publicly available information that can be freely accessed, analyzed, and utilized for intelligence purposes, this includes sources such as news articles, social media posts, online forums, blogs, and government reports, organizations can harness open source data to supplement their internal threat intelligence efforts and gain insights into the tactics, techniques, and procedures (TTPs) used by threat actors, one common approach is monitoring social media platforms for discussions, announcements, or bragging about cyber attacks, threat actors often use social media to communicate with each other, share tools and resources, or publicize their exploits, analysts can use social media monitoring tools such as Hootsuite or TweetDeck to track relevant keywords, hashtags, or accounts associated with cyber threats, enabling them to identify new threats, trends, or indicators of compromise (IOCs), another valuable source of open source data is security blogs and research papers, cybersecurity researchers and experts often publish their findings, analysis, and insights into emerging threats, vulnerabilities, and attack techniques, organizations can follow reputable security blogs such as Krebs on Security, Threatpost, or the SANS Internet Storm Center to stay informed about the latest developments in the threat landscape, moreover, threat intelligence platforms (TIPs) can aggregate and analyze open source data from various sources, enabling organizations to correlate and contextualize information to identify relevant threats and prioritize their response, TIPs such as ThreatConnect, Recorded Future, or Anomali offer features such as data ingestion, enrichment, and visualization, allowing analysts to make informed decisions based on comprehensive threat intelligence, additionally, open source intelligence (OSINT) gathering techniques can provide valuable insights into the infrastructure and activities of threat actors, OSINT involves collecting and analyzing publicly available information from a wide range of sources, including websites, domain registries, WHOIS databases, and online repositories, analysts can use tools such as Maltego, Shodan, or SpiderFoot to gather information about domain ownership, IP addresses, SSL certificates, or exposed services, enabling them to map out the attack surface and identify potential vulnerabilities or misconfigurations, furthermore, dark web monitoring can uncover hidden forums, marketplaces, or communication channels used by threat actors to buy, sell, or exchange malicious tools and services, organizations can use specialized dark web monitoring tools such as DarkOwl or Flashpoint to search for mentions of their organization, employees, or sensitive data on the dark web, enabling them to detect potential breaches or data leaks early, however, it is essential to exercise caution when collecting and analyzing open source data, as it may contain inaccurate, misleading, or biased information, analysts should verify the credibility and reliability of their sources and cross-reference information from multiple sources to validate its accuracy, moreover, organizations must also consider legal and ethical considerations when collecting open source data, particularly when accessing sensitive or private information, compliance with data protection regulations such as the General Data Protection Regulation (GDPR) or the California Consumer Privacy Act (CCPA) is paramount to avoid legal repercussions, organizations should establish clear policies and procedures for collecting, storing, and handling open source data in compliance with applicable laws and regulations, finally, collaboration and information sharing among organizations, government agencies, and industry partners can enhance the effectiveness of open source threat intelligence efforts, by sharing insights, best practices, and lessons learned, organizations can collectively identify and respond to emerging threats more effectively, enabling them to better protect their assets, data, and reputation from cyber attacks. OSINT tools and techniques are invaluable resources for cybersecurity professionals seeking to gather intelligence from publicly available sources, OSINT, or Open Source Intelligence, encompasses a wide range of methods and tools for collecting, analyzing, and leveraging information from publicly accessible sources, these sources include websites, social media platforms, online forums, public records, and more, one widely used OSINT tool is Maltego, which allows analysts to visualize and map out relationships between entities such as domains, IP addresses, and individuals, analysts can use Maltego to gather information about a target's online presence, identify potential connections or associations, and uncover hidden relationships, another popular OSINT tool is Shodan, a search engine that scans the internet for devices and services, Shodan allows analysts to search for specific devices, such as webcams, routers, or servers, and gather information about their configurations, vulnerabilities, and potential security risks, moreover, analysts can use SpiderFoot to automate the process of collecting OSINT data from multiple sources, SpiderFoot gathers information from websites, DNS records, social media platforms, and other sources, and presents it in a unified dashboard for analysis, enabling analysts to quickly identify relevant information and connections, additionally, analysts can use FOCA (Fingerprinting Organizations with Collected Archives) to extract metadata from documents and files found on websites or servers, FOCA can identify document authorship, software versions, and network infrastructure details, providing valuable insights into a target's environment, furthermore, analysts can leverage social media monitoring tools such as Hootsuite or TweetDeck to track mentions of keywords, hashtags, or accounts related to their investigation, social media platforms like Twitter, Facebook, and LinkedIn are rich sources of information about individuals, organizations, events, and trends, analysts can monitor social media for discussions, announcements, or indicators of compromise (IOCs) related to cyber threats, allowing them to stay ahead of emerging threats, moreover, analysts can use WHOIS lookup tools to gather information about domain registrations, WHOIS databases contain information about domain owners, registration dates, contact details, and more, analysts can use WHOIS lookup tools such as WHOIS or ICANN Lookup to query domain registration records and gather intelligence about potential threat actors or malicious domains, additionally, analysts can use domain reputation services such as VirusTotal or DomainTools to assess the reputation and trustworthiness of domains, these services analyze domain attributes, historical data, and associations with malicious activity to determine whether a domain is trustworthy or potentially malicious, furthermore, analysts can use web scraping tools such as Scrapy or Beautiful Soup to extract data from websites, web scraping allows analysts to collect information from web pages, forums, or online databases in a structured format for analysis, enabling them to uncover hidden insights or patterns, finally, analysts must exercise caution and adhere to legal and ethical guidelines when conducting OSINT activities, analysts should respect privacy laws and regulations, obtain consent when necessary, and avoid accessing or disseminating sensitive or confidential information without authorization, by leveraging OSINT tools and techniques responsibly, analysts can gather valuable intelligence to support their cybersecurity investigations and enhance their organization's security posture.

Chapter 5: Dark Web Monitoring and Analysis

Exploring the Dark Web for threat intelligence is a complex yet valuable endeavor for cybersecurity professionals seeking insights into underground activities and emerging threats, the Dark Web, a hidden portion of the internet not indexed by traditional search engines, hosts a plethora of illicit marketplaces, forums, and communication channels frequented by cybercriminals, activists, and other nefarious actors, accessing the Dark Web requires specialized tools and techniques to navigate its anonymized and encrypted infrastructure, one commonly used tool for accessing the Dark Web is the Tor browser, which enables users to browse websites hosted on the Tor network anonymously, Tor routes internet traffic through a series of encrypted relays to conceal a user's identity and location, allowing users to access websites on the Dark Web without revealing their IP address, another approach to accessing the Dark Web is through virtual private networks (VPNs), VPNs encrypt internet traffic and route it through remote servers, obscuring the user's IP address and location, this can provide an additional layer of anonymity when accessing Dark Web sites, however, it is essential to use reputable VPN services to ensure privacy and security, moreover, once connected to the Tor network, users can explore Dark Web marketplaces, forums, and communication channels to gather intelligence on various cyber threats, marketplaces such as AlphaBay, Empire Market, and Silk Road 3.0 host listings for illicit goods and services, including stolen data, drugs, malware, and hacking tools, analysts can monitor these marketplaces to track the sale of sensitive information, identify emerging threats, and assess the demand for cybercriminal services, additionally, Dark Web forums and chat rooms serve as hubs for cybercriminals to exchange knowledge, collaborate on attacks, and recruit new members, analysts can infiltrate these communities to gather intelligence on threat actors, their tactics, and their targets, however, it is essential to exercise caution and avoid engaging in illegal activities or compromising operational security, furthermore, Dark Web intelligence gathering can uncover indicators of compromise (IOCs) and threat actor infrastructure that may be used in cyber attacks, analysts can identify malicious domains, IP addresses, and email addresses associated with phishing campaigns, malware distribution, or command and control servers, allowing organizations to proactively defend against cyber threats, moreover, Dark Web monitoring tools such as DarkOwl or Flashpoint provide automated capabilities for collecting and analyzing Dark Web data, these tools can search for mentions of an organization's name, employees, or sensitive data on Dark Web forums and marketplaces, enabling organizations to detect potential breaches or data leaks early, however, organizations must balance the benefits of Dark Web intelligence gathering with legal and ethical considerations, accessing and monitoring the Dark Web may involve navigating a legal gray area and could potentially expose organizations to legal risks, analysts should adhere to applicable laws and regulations, obtain proper authorization, and avoid engaging in activities that could violate privacy or compromise security, In summary, exploring the Dark Web for threat intelligence requires specialized tools, techniques, and expertise, but it can provide valuable insights into underground activities, emerging threats, and cybercriminal behavior, by leveraging Dark Web intelligence responsibly, organizations can enhance their cybersecurity posture and mitigate the risks posed by cyber threats. Dark Web monitoring strategies are essential for organizations aiming to proactively detect and mitigate cyber threats originating from underground networks and illicit marketplaces, monitoring the Dark Web involves systematically tracking and analyzing online activities within hidden forums, marketplaces, and communication channels frequented by cybercriminals and threat actors, these strategies enable organizations to identify potential threats, vulnerabilities, and breaches that may impact their security posture, one key aspect of Dark Web monitoring is the use of specialized tools and technologies to collect and analyze data from Dark Web sources, analysts can utilize Dark Web intelligence platforms such as DarkOwl, Flashpoint, or Recorded Future to automate the process of gathering information from underground forums, marketplaces, and chat rooms, these platforms aggregate data from various Dark Web sources and provide analysts with insights into emerging threats, malicious activities, and indicators of compromise (IOCs), enabling organizations to stay ahead of cyber threats, moreover, analysts can deploy web crawlers and scrapers to collect data from Dark Web sites and forums, web crawlers navigate through Dark Web pages, indexing content and extracting relevant information such as forum posts, listings, and discussions, this data can then be analyzed for potential threats or vulnerabilities, furthermore, organizations can establish partnerships with law enforcement agencies, cybersecurity firms, and threat intelligence providers to access shared repositories of Dark Web data and intelligence, these partnerships enable organizations to leverage the collective expertise and resources of the cybersecurity community to enhance their threat detection capabilities, additionally, organizations can deploy honeypots and decoy accounts on the Dark Web to lure and track cybercriminal activity, honeypots mimic legitimate services or resources, attracting attackers and allowing organizations to monitor their tactics, techniques, and procedures (TTPs), decoy accounts can be used to infiltrate Dark Web forums and communities, enabling analysts to gather intelligence on threat actors and their activities, moreover, organizations can implement automated monitoring and alerting systems to detect and respond to suspicious activity on the Dark Web, these systems continuously monitor Dark Web sources for keywords, indicators, or patterns indicative of cyber threats, such as mentions of the organization's name, employee credentials, or stolen data, when suspicious activity is detected, alerts are generated, enabling organizations to investigate and respond promptly, furthermore, organizations must establish clear policies and procedures for handling Dark Web intelligence, including protocols for sharing information with relevant stakeholders, responding to threats, and maintaining confidentiality, it is essential to ensure that Dark Web monitoring activities comply with legal and ethical guidelines, including privacy laws, data protection regulations, and law enforcement requirements, organizations should prioritize transparency, accountability, and respect for individual privacy rights when conducting Dark Web monitoring, In summary, Dark Web monitoring strategies are vital components of an organization's cybersecurity strategy, enabling proactive threat detection, intelligence gathering, and response capabilities, by leveraging specialized tools, technologies, and partnerships, organizations can effectively mitigate the risks posed by cyber threats originating from underground networks and illicit marketplaces.

Chapter 6: Indicators of Compromise (IOCs) and Threat Feeds

Identifying indicators of compromise (IOCs) is crucial in modern cybersecurity to detect and respond to potential security incidents and breaches, IOCs are artifacts or patterns of activity that indicate a system has been compromised or is under attack, they can include file hashes, IP addresses, domain names, registry keys, or patterns of behavior associated with malicious activity, one common method for identifying IOCs is through the analysis of system logs and network traffic, security analysts can use tools such as Splunk, ELK Stack, or Graylog to collect, parse, and analyze logs from various sources, including servers, endpoints, firewalls, and intrusion detection systems (IDS), these tools enable analysts to search for known IOCs or unusual patterns of activity that may indicate a security breach, moreover, organizations can leverage threat intelligence feeds to identify IOCs associated with known threats or attack campaigns, threat intelligence platforms such as ThreatConnect, Anomali, or AlienVault provide curated feeds of IOCs collected from various sources, including open-source intelligence, commercial threat intelligence providers, and community contributions, these feeds can be integrated into security systems to automatically block or alert on traffic associated with known threats, furthermore, endpoint detection and response (EDR) solutions play a critical role in identifying IOCs on individual devices, EDR agents monitor endpoint activity in real-time, collecting data on process execution, file modifications, network connections, and other behaviors indicative of compromise, they can detect malware infections, suspicious file downloads, unauthorized access attempts, or other signs of malicious activity, organizations can deploy EDR solutions such as CrowdStrike Falcon, Carbon Black, or SentinelOne to monitor and respond to threats across their endpoint environment, additionally, organizations can conduct threat hunting activities to proactively search for IOCs and signs of compromise within their network, threat hunters use a combination of automated tools, manual analysis, and human expertise to search for anomalous activity or indicators that may have evaded traditional security controls, they analyze log data, network traffic, and endpoint telemetry to identify signs of compromise, such as unusual file access patterns, unauthorized user accounts, or abnormal network behavior, moreover, organizations can leverage security information and event management (SIEM) systems to correlate and analyze data from multiple sources to identify potential IOCs, SIEM platforms such as Splunk, QRadar, or ArcSight aggregate log and event data from across the organization's IT infrastructure, enabling analysts to detect and investigate security incidents, they use correlation rules, threat intelligence feeds, and machine learning algorithms to identify patterns indicative of malicious activity, finally, organizations must establish robust incident response procedures to effectively respond to identified IOCs, incident response teams must be trained to quickly assess the severity of a potential breach, contain the threat, and remediate affected systems to minimize damage and prevent further spread, they should follow predefined playbooks and escalation procedures to ensure a coordinated and efficient response, collaborating with internal stakeholders, external partners, and law enforcement as needed, In summary, identifying indicators of compromise is a critical aspect of modern cybersecurity, enabling organizations to detect and respond to security incidents in a timely manner, by leveraging a combination of tools, technologies, and human expertise, organizations can effectively identify and mitigate the impact of security breaches and protect their digital assets. Utilizing threat intelligence feeds is a fundamental aspect of modern cybersecurity strategy, threat intelligence feeds provide organizations with timely and relevant information about emerging threats, vulnerabilities, and malicious activities, they enable organizations to enhance their security posture by proactively identifying and mitigating potential risks, one common type of threat intelligence feed is the IP blacklist, IP blacklists contain lists of known malicious IP addresses that have been associated with malicious activity, such as malware distribution, phishing attacks, or command and control servers, organizations can leverage IP blacklists to block traffic from known malicious sources at the network perimeter, thereby reducing the risk of successful cyber attacks, for example, organizations can use the "iptables" command on Linux-based systems to create firewall rules that block traffic from specific IP addresses listed in a threat intelligence feed, by regularly updating their firewall rules with the latest IP blacklists, organizations can effectively block traffic from known malicious sources, another type of threat intelligence feed is the domain blacklist, domain blacklists contain lists of known malicious domain names that have been associated with phishing, malware distribution, or other malicious activities, organizations can use domain blacklists to block access to known malicious websites or prevent users from receiving emails containing malicious links, for example, organizations can configure their DNS servers to block access to domains listed in a threat intelligence feed using tools such as BIND or Microsoft DNS, by configuring DNS blacklisting, organizations can prevent users from accessing known malicious domains and reduce the risk of falling victim to phishing or malware attacks, moreover, some threat intelligence feeds provide information about specific malware samples, such as file hashes, file names, or indicators of compromise (IOCs), organizations can use this information to detect and remove malware infections from their systems, for example, organizations can use the "md5sum" or "sha256sum" commands on Linux-based systems to calculate the hash value of a file and compare it to known malicious hashes listed in a threat intelligence feed, if a match is found, it indicates that the file may be malicious and should be investigated further, additionally, some threat intelligence feeds provide information about vulnerabilities in software or hardware products, organizations can use this information to prioritize patching and remediation efforts, for example, organizations can use the "nmap" command to scan their network for systems running vulnerable software versions and compare the results to vulnerability information provided in a threat intelligence feed, by identifying systems that are vulnerable to known exploits, organizations can prioritize patching and apply security updates to reduce the risk of exploitation, furthermore, threat intelligence feeds can provide organizations with information about emerging threats and attack trends, enabling them to adapt their security defenses accordingly, for example, organizations can use threat intelligence feeds to identify new attack techniques, tactics, and procedures (TTPs) used by threat actors, they can then adjust their security controls and incident response procedures to better detect and respond to these emerging threats, ultimately, threat intelligence feeds play a crucial role in helping organizations stay ahead of cyber threats and protect their digital assets, by leveraging the wealth of information provided by threat intelligence feeds, organizations can enhance their security posture, improve their incident response capabilities, and mitigate the risks posed by cyber attacks.

Chapter 7: Threat Intelligence Platforms (TIPs) and Tools

An overview of threat intelligence platforms reveals their pivotal role in modern cybersecurity operations, threat intelligence platforms (TIPs) serve as centralized repositories for collecting, analyzing, and disseminating threat intelligence data, they enable organizations to aggregate information from various sources, such as open-source feeds, commercial vendors, internal sources, and community contributions, and correlate it to identify emerging threats and vulnerabilities, one key feature of TIPs is their ability to automate the collection and normalization of threat intelligence data, TIPs can ingest data from a wide range of sources, including feeds of indicators of compromise (IOCs), vulnerability information, threat actor profiles, and security advisories, they use standard formats such as STIX/TAXII or OpenIOC to normalize the data, making it easier to correlate and analyze across different sources, for example, organizations can use the "taxii-client" command-line tool to retrieve threat intelligence data from a TAXII server and import it into their TIP, by automating the collection and normalization process, TIPs enable organizations to stay up-to-date with the latest threat intelligence without manual intervention, another key feature of TIPs is their ability to correlate and analyze threat intelligence data to identify patterns and trends, TIPs use advanced analytics and machine learning algorithms to detect anomalies and suspicious activity in large volumes of data, for example, organizations can use the "analyze" command in their TIP to perform statistical analysis on threat intelligence data and identify correlations between different types of threats, by analyzing threat intelligence data in real-time, TIPs enable organizations to detect and respond to threats more quickly, furthermore, TIPs provide organizations with tools for enriching threat intelligence data with additional context and information, TIPs can integrate with external sources such as vulnerability scanners, security information and event management (SIEM) systems, and intrusion detection systems (IDS), to enrich threat intelligence data with additional context, for example, organizations can use the "enrich" command in their TIP to enrich IOCs with information about related vulnerabilities, malware samples, or threat actor profiles, by enriching threat intelligence data, organizations can better understand the potential impact of threats and prioritize their response efforts, moreover, TIPs enable organizations to share threat intelligence data with trusted partners and industry peers, TIPs support standards such as STIX/TAXII and MISP for sharing threat intelligence data in a standardized format, organizations can use the "share" command in their TIP to exchange threat intelligence data with other organizations, such as industry information sharing and analysis centers (ISACs) or government agencies, by sharing threat intelligence data, organizations can collaborate more effectively to identify and mitigate cyber threats, additionally, TIPs provide organizations with capabilities for managing and operationalizing threat intelligence data, TIPs offer features such as case management, workflow automation, and integration with incident response processes, for example, organizations can use the "create-case" command in their TIP to create a new incident response case for investigating a potential security incident, by integrating threat intelligence data with incident response processes, organizations can streamline their response efforts and reduce the time to detect and mitigate threats, In summary, threat intelligence platforms play a critical role in modern cybersecurity operations, enabling organizations to collect, analyze, and operationalize threat intelligence data to protect against cyber threats, by leveraging the capabilities of TIPs, organizations can enhance their security posture, improve their incident response capabilities, and mitigate the risks posed by cyber attacks. Evaluation and selection of Threat Intelligence Platforms (TIPs) is a critical process for organizations seeking to enhance their cybersecurity capabilities, when evaluating TIPs, organizations should consider a range of factors, including their specific requirements, budget constraints, and technical capabilities, one important consideration is the range of data sources supported by the TIP, organizations should look for TIPs that can ingest threat intelligence data from a variety of sources, such as open-source feeds, commercial vendors, and internal sources, ensuring that the TIP can integrate with existing security infrastructure is also essential, organizations should assess the TIP's compatibility with their existing security tools, such as SIEM systems, IDS/IPS solutions, and endpoint security platforms, by selecting a TIP that integrates seamlessly with existing tools, organizations can streamline their threat intelligence workflows and improve their overall security posture, furthermore, organizations should evaluate the scalability and performance of TIPs, particularly for large enterprises or those with high-volume threat intelligence needs, it is essential to ensure that the TIP can handle the volume of data generated by the organization and provide timely analysis and response capabilities, conducting thorough performance testing and scalability assessments can help organizations identify potential limitations and ensure that the selected TIP can meet their needs, another important factor to consider is the usability and ease of use of the TIP, organizations should evaluate the TIP's user interface, reporting capabilities, and customization options to ensure that it meets the needs of their security teams, providing training and support for security analysts can also help organizations maximize the value of their TIP investment, in addition to technical considerations, organizations should also assess the vendor's reputation, track record, and customer support capabilities, selecting a reputable vendor with a proven track record of delivering high-quality products and responsive support can help mitigate risks and ensure a successful implementation, conducting reference checks and seeking feedback from existing customers can provide valuable insights into the vendor's reliability and customer service, moreover, organizations should evaluate the TIP's threat intelligence capabilities, including its ability to correlate and analyze threat intelligence data, detect and prioritize threats, and provide actionable insights to security teams, features such as automated threat detection, threat scoring, and incident response orchestration can significantly enhance organizations' ability to detect and respond to cyber threats, conducting a comprehensive evaluation of TIPs against these criteria can help organizations identify the most suitable solution for their needs, ultimately, selecting the right TIP is crucial for organizations looking to improve their cybersecurity posture and effectively defend against increasingly sophisticated cyber threats, by carefully evaluating and selecting TIPs that meet their requirements, organizations can enhance their threat intelligence capabilities, improve their incident response processes, and better protect their digital assets.

Chapter 8: Threat Hunting Methodologies

Proactive threat detection strategies are essential components of modern cybersecurity programs, they involve the continuous monitoring of networks, systems, and applications to identify potential security threats before they can cause harm, one key proactive threat detection strategy is the implementation of intrusion detection systems (IDS), IDS are security tools that monitor network traffic for suspicious activity or known attack patterns, they can detect a wide range of threats, including malware infections, unauthorized access attempts, and denial-of-service attacks, organizations can deploy IDS sensors at key points in their network infrastructure to monitor traffic and alert security teams to potential threats, for example, organizations can use the "snort" command to deploy the Snort IDS on their network and configure it to monitor traffic for specific signatures or anomalies, by deploying IDS, organizations can detect and respond to security threats in real-time, another proactive threat detection strategy is the use of endpoint detection and response (EDR) solutions, EDR solutions are security tools that monitor endpoint devices, such as laptops, desktops, and servers, for signs of malicious activity, they can detect suspicious behavior, such as file changes, registry modifications, and process executions, and alert security teams to potential threats, organizations can deploy EDR agents on endpoint devices to continuously monitor for security incidents, for example, organizations can use the "carbon-black" command to deploy Carbon Black EDR agents on their endpoint devices and configure them to report suspicious activity to a central management console, by deploying EDR solutions, organizations can improve their visibility into endpoint security threats and respond more effectively to security incidents, furthermore, organizations can use threat hunting as a proactive threat detection strategy, threat hunting involves actively searching for signs of malicious activity within an organization's network and systems, it complements traditional security monitoring by allowing security teams to proactively identify and investigate potential threats, organizations can use a variety of techniques and tools to conduct threat hunting, including log analysis, network traffic analysis, and endpoint forensics, for example, organizations can use the "splunk" command to search through log data for indicators of compromise or use the "wireshark" command to analyze network traffic for signs of suspicious activity, by conducting regular threat hunting exercises, organizations can identify and mitigate security threats before they can cause damage, moreover, organizations can use threat intelligence as part of their proactive threat detection strategy, threat intelligence involves collecting, analyzing, and disseminating information about current and emerging security threats, organizations can use threat intelligence to identify potential threats and vulnerabilities in their environment and take proactive steps to mitigate them, for example, organizations can use the "misp" command to integrate threat intelligence feeds into their security tools and correlate threat intelligence data with security events, by leveraging threat intelligence, organizations can stay ahead of evolving security threats and better protect their assets, In summary, proactive threat detection strategies are essential for organizations looking to defend against increasingly sophisticated cyber threats, by implementing intrusion detection systems, endpoint detection and response solutions, threat hunting techniques, and leveraging threat intelligence, organizations can improve their ability to detect and respond to security threats proactively. Threat hunting techniques and frameworks play a crucial role in modern cybersecurity practices, they involve proactive and systematic searches for potential security threats within an organization's network and systems, threat hunting goes beyond traditional security monitoring by actively seeking out indicators of compromise and signs of malicious activity, organizations can use a variety of techniques and frameworks to conduct threat hunting effectively, one commonly used approach is the Cyber Kill Chain framework, developed by Lockheed Martin, the Cyber Kill Chain breaks down the stages of a cyber attack into distinct phases, including reconnaissance, weaponization, delivery, exploitation, installation, command and control, and actions on objectives, by understanding each phase of the attack lifecycle, organizations can develop proactive strategies to detect and mitigate threats, for example, organizations can use the "mitre-attack" command to access the MITRE ATT&CK framework, which provides a comprehensive matrix of adversary tactics, techniques, and procedures, organizations can use the MITRE ATT&CK framework to map observed behaviors to specific attack techniques and identify gaps in their defenses, another popular threat hunting technique is anomaly detection, anomaly detection involves identifying deviations from normal behavior within an organization's network and systems, anomalies may indicate the presence of malicious activity or security threats, organizations can use machine learning algorithms and statistical analysis techniques to identify anomalies and prioritize them for further investigation, for example, organizations can use the "elastic-stack" command to deploy the Elastic Stack, which includes Elasticsearch, Logstash, and Kibana, organizations can use Elasticsearch to index and search log data, Logstash to collect and parse log files, and Kibana to visualize and analyze log data for anomalies, by leveraging anomaly detection techniques, organizations can proactively identify and respond to security threats, furthermore, threat hunting often involves the use of threat intelligence, threat intelligence provides organizations with information about current and emerging security threats, including tactics, techniques, and procedures used by cyber adversaries, organizations can use threat intelligence to identify potential threats and prioritize their threat hunting efforts, for example, organizations can use the "alienvault" command to deploy AlienVault USM, which includes threat intelligence feeds from AlienVault's Open Threat Exchange (OTX), organizations can use OTX to access real-time threat intelligence data and correlate it with security events to identify potential threats, by leveraging threat intelligence, organizations can enhance their threat hunting capabilities and stay ahead of evolving security threats, moreover, threat hunting requires skilled personnel with expertise in cybersecurity and threat analysis, organizations should invest in training and development programs to build a team of skilled threat hunters, for example, organizations can provide training on threat hunting techniques, tools, and frameworks, as well as hands-on experience with real-world security incidents, by investing in their people, organizations can build a capable and effective threat hunting team, In summary, threat hunting techniques and frameworks are essential for organizations looking to proactively detect and respond to security threats, by leveraging techniques such as the Cyber Kill Chain framework, anomaly detection, and threat intelligence, organizations can improve their ability to identify and mitigate security threats before they can cause damage.

Chapter 9: Incident Response with Threat Intelligence Integration

Integrating threat intelligence into incident response is paramount in modern cybersecurity practices, it enables organizations to effectively detect, respond to, and mitigate security incidents, incident response teams can leverage threat intelligence to gain insights into the tactics, techniques, and procedures (TTPs) used by adversaries, this information can help teams prioritize and contextualize security alerts, enabling faster and more accurate incident response, one way to integrate threat intelligence into incident response is through the use of threat intelligence platforms (TIPs), TIPs aggregate, correlate, and analyze threat intelligence data from various sources, allowing incident response teams to access timely and relevant threat information, organizations can use TIPs to enrich security alerts with additional context from threat intelligence feeds, for example, organizations can use the "alienvault" command to deploy AlienVault USM, which includes a built-in threat intelligence platform, incident response teams can use AlienVault USM to correlate security events with threat intelligence data from AlienVault's

Open Threat Exchange (OTX), this allows teams to quickly identify and respond to security incidents based on known threat indicators, another way to integrate threat intelligence into incident response is through the use of threat intelligence feeds, threat intelligence feeds provide organizations with real-time information about emerging threats and malicious activity, organizations can subscribe to threat intelligence feeds from commercial vendors, open-source projects, and government agencies, for example, organizations can use the "cisco-amp" command to deploy Cisco Advanced Malware Protection (AMP), which includes threat intelligence feeds from Cisco Talos, incident response teams can use Cisco AMP to block known malicious files and URLs based on threat intelligence from Cisco Talos, this helps organizations prevent security incidents before they occur, furthermore, organizations can integrate threat intelligence into their incident response playbooks and workflows, incident response playbooks outline step-by-step procedures for responding to specific types of security incidents, organizations can use threat intelligence to enhance their playbooks with additional context and response actions, for example, organizations can create playbook actions that automatically block malicious IP addresses or quarantine compromised devices based on threat intelligence indicators, this helps streamline incident response processes and reduce manual effort, moreover, organizations can use threat intelligence to improve post-incident analysis and remediation efforts, threat intelligence data collected during incident response can provide valuable insights into the tactics and techniques used by adversaries, organizations can use this information to update their security controls, fine-tune their incident response procedures, and improve their overall security posture, for example, organizations can use threat intelligence data to identify gaps in their defenses and prioritize remediation efforts based on the most critical threats, by integrating threat intelligence into incident response, organizations can enhance their ability to detect, respond to, and recover from security incidents in a timely and effective manner. Threat intelligence-driven incident response workflows are essential for organizations to effectively detect, respond to, and mitigate security incidents, these workflows leverage threat intelligence to enhance incident detection, analysis, and response activities, incident response teams can use threat intelligence to identify and prioritize security incidents based on the severity of the threats they pose, this allows teams to focus their resources and efforts on the most critical incidents, organizations can use threat intelligence platforms (TIPs) to automate the ingestion, enrichment, and correlation of threat intelligence data with security event data from their networks, for example, organizations can use the "alienvault" command to deploy AlienVault USM, a unified security management platform that includes built-in threat intelligence capabilities, incident response teams can use AlienVault USM to automatically correlate security events with threat intelligence data from AlienVault's Open Threat Exchange (OTX), enabling faster and more accurate incident response, in addition to TIPs, organizations can leverage threat intelligence feeds to enrich their incident response workflows with real-time threat information, threat intelligence feeds provide organizations with up-to-date information about emerging threats, malicious actors, and attack techniques, incident response teams can subscribe to threat intelligence feeds from commercial vendors, open-source projects, and government agencies, for example, organizations can use the "cisco-amp" command to deploy Cisco Advanced Malware Protection (AMP), which includes threat intelligence feeds from Cisco Talos, incident response teams can use Cisco AMP to block known malicious files and URLs based on threat intelligence from Cisco Talos, this helps organizations prevent security incidents before they occur, furthermore, threat intelligence-driven incident response workflows can help organizations improve their incident detection capabilities, incident response teams can use threat intelligence to create custom detection rules and signatures that are tailored to their organization's specific threat landscape, for example, organizations can use threat intelligence data to create intrusion detection system (IDS) rules that detect known indicators of compromise (IOCs), such as malicious IP addresses, domains, and file hashes, incident response teams can then use these rules to automatically alert on and investigate suspicious activity, moreover, threat intelligence-driven incident response workflows can enable organizations to respond to security incidents more effectively, incident response teams can use threat intelligence to guide their response actions and prioritize remediation efforts, for example, organizations can use threat intelligence data to identify the root cause of a security incident and determine the appropriate response actions, incident response teams can then use this information to contain the incident, eradicate any malicious activity, and restore affected systems to a secure state, by leveraging threat intelligence-driven incident response workflows, organizations can enhance their ability to detect, respond to, and recover from security incidents in a timely and effective manner.

Chapter 10: Cyber Threat Forecasting and Trends Analysis

Predictive analysis in cyber threat forecasting plays a crucial role in helping organizations anticipate and prepare for potential security threats and attacks, this approach involves analyzing historical data, current trends, and emerging patterns to forecast future cyber threats, organizations can use predictive analysis to identify potential vulnerabilities, anticipate attack vectors, and develop proactive security measures to mitigate risks, by leveraging predictive analysis, organizations can stay one step ahead of cyber attackers and minimize the impact of security incidents, to deploy predictive analysis techniques, organizations can use machine learning algorithms to analyze large volumes of security data and identify patterns and anomalies that may indicate potential security threats, for example, organizations can use the "python" command to deploy machine learning frameworks such as scikit-learn or TensorFlow, incident response teams can then use these frameworks to train predictive models using historical security data, including information about past security incidents, attack patterns, and indicators of compromise (IOCs), once trained, these models can be used to analyze real-time security data and identify potential security threats, organizations can also use predictive analysis to prioritize security resources and focus on addressing the most critical risks, for example, organizations can use predictive models to assign risk scores to different assets and prioritize security measures based on the level of risk they pose, this allows organizations to allocate resources more efficiently and effectively, furthermore, predictive analysis can help organizations improve their incident response capabilities by enabling faster and more accurate detection of security incidents, for example, organizations can use predictive models to analyze network traffic data and identify abnormal patterns or behaviors that may indicate a security breach, incident response teams can then use this information to investigate and respond to security incidents more quickly, reducing the time to detect and contain threats, moreover, predictive analysis can help organizations identify emerging cyber threats and adapt their security strategies accordingly, for example, organizations can use predictive models to analyze threat intelligence data and identify new attack vectors or malware variants that may pose a risk to their environment, incident response teams can then use this information to update their security controls and defenses to protect against these emerging threats, by incorporating predictive analysis into their cybersecurity programs, organizations can enhance their ability to anticipate, detect, and respond to cyber threats in a proactive and effective manner, this can help organizations reduce the likelihood and impact of security incidents, protect sensitive data and assets, and maintain the trust and confidence of their customers and stakeholders, overall, predictive analysis is a valuable tool for organizations seeking to stay ahead of evolving cyber threats and maintain a strong security posture in today's dynamic threat landscape. Analyzing future cyber threat trends is essential for organizations to anticipate and prepare for emerging security challenges, this involves examining current cybersecurity landscape and extrapolating potential future threats based on technological advancements, threat actor tactics, and evolving attack vectors, by understanding emerging cyber threat trends, organizations can develop proactive strategies to mitigate risks and enhance their cybersecurity posture, to analyze future cyber threat trends, organizations can leverage threat intelligence platforms (TIPs) and security information and event management (SIEM) tools to aggregate and analyze vast amounts of security data, for instance, they can use the "grep" command to search for specific threat indicators or patterns within log files or network traffic data, furthermore, organizations can monitor industry-specific forums, security blogs, and information sharing communities to stay abreast of emerging cyber threats and attack techniques, they can use the "curl" command to retrieve information from threat intelligence feeds or online forums, by closely monitoring these sources, organizations can gain insights into new attack methodologies, vulnerabilities, and exploits that may pose a risk to their environment, moreover, organizations can conduct scenario-based risk assessments and tabletop exercises to simulate potential cyber threats and assess their readiness to respond, they can use the "nmap" command to scan their network for vulnerabilities and identify potential attack vectors, by simulating realistic cyber threat scenarios, organizations can identify gaps in their security controls and processes and take proactive measures to address them, additionally, organizations can collaborate with industry peers, government agencies, and cybersecurity vendors to share threat intelligence and best practices for mitigating emerging cyber threats, they can use the "ssh" command to securely connect to external partners' systems and exchange information, by sharing threat intelligence and collaborating with trusted partners, organizations can gain valuable insights into emerging cyber threats and strengthen their collective defenses, furthermore, organizations can leverage machine learning and artificial intelligence (AI) algorithms to analyze large datasets and identify patterns and anomalies that may indicate future cyber threats, they can use the "tensorflow" command to deploy machine learning models for predictive analysis, by harnessing the power of AI and machine learning, organizations can enhance their ability to detect and respond to emerging cyber threats in real time, moreover, organizations can implement proactive security measures such as threat hunting and penetration testing to identify potential vulnerabilities and weaknesses in their environment before they can be exploited by threat actors, they can use the "metasploit" framework to simulate real-world cyber attacks and assess their defenses, by proactively identifying and addressing security weaknesses, organizations can reduce the likelihood and impact of future cyber threats, overall, analyzing future cyber threat trends is essential for organizations to stay ahead of evolving security risks and protect their assets and data from cyber attacks.

BOOK 4
MASTERING INCIDENT RESPONSE
EXPERT TACTICS FOR CYSA+ EXAM CS0-003

ROB BOTWRIGHT

Chapter 1: Incident Response Fundamentals

Understanding incident response frameworks is crucial for organizations to effectively manage and mitigate cybersecurity incidents, incident response frameworks provide structured guidelines and procedures for responding to security incidents in a systematic and organized manner, one of the most widely adopted incident response frameworks is the NIST Computer Security Incident Handling Guide (NIST SP 800-61), developed by the National Institute of Standards and Technology (NIST), this framework outlines a step-by-step approach to incident response, including preparation, detection and analysis, containment, eradication, and recovery, organizations can use the NIST incident response framework to establish formal incident response policies and procedures tailored to their specific needs and requirements, another commonly used incident response framework is the SANS Institute's Incident Handler's Handbook, which offers practical guidance and best practices for incident response teams, including incident detection and classification, escalation procedures, and post-incident analysis, incident response frameworks typically follow a cyclical process known as the "incident response lifecycle," which consists of six phases: preparation, identification, containment, eradication, recovery, and lessons learned, during the preparation phase, organizations develop and implement incident response plans, establish communication channels, and train incident response teams, they can use the "cp" command to make copies of critical system files and configuration files for backup purposes, in the identification phase, organizations detect and classify security incidents by monitoring network traffic, analyzing log files, and deploying intrusion detection systems (IDS), they can use the "grep" command to search for specific keywords or patterns in log files, in the containment phase, organizations take immediate actions to limit the impact of security incidents and prevent further damage, this may involve isolating compromised systems from the network, blocking malicious IP addresses, or disabling compromised user accounts, they can use the "iptables" command to configure firewall rules to block suspicious network traffic, in the eradication phase, organizations remove malware, patch vulnerabilities, and restore affected systems to a secure state, they can use the "rm" command to delete malicious files and directories from infected systems, in the recovery phase, organizations restore normal operations and data from backups, they can use the "rsync" command to synchronize data between backup servers and production systems, finally, in the lessons learned phase, organizations conduct post-incident analysis to identify weaknesses in their incident response processes and make improvements for future incidents, they can use the "grep" command to search for specific incident-related events in log files and analyze the root causes of security incidents, overall, understanding incident response frameworks is essential for organizations to effectively detect, respond to, and recover from cybersecurity incidents in a timely and efficient manner. Key components of incident response encompass various elements crucial for effectively addressing cybersecurity incidents within an organization, these components include incident detection and classification, which involve identifying and categorizing security incidents based on their severity and impact on the organization's assets and operations, incident detection often relies on tools such as intrusion detection systems (IDS) and security information and event management (SIEM) solutions, which monitor network traffic and log data for signs of suspicious activity, organizations can use the "tcpdump" command to capture network packets for analysis and the "tail" command to monitor log files in real-time, incident classification involves assessing the nature and scope of the incident to determine the appropriate response actions, organizations can use the "grep" command to search for specific indicators of compromise (IOCs) in log files and security alerts, another key component is incident triage and prioritization, which involves assessing the urgency and criticality of security incidents to allocate resources effectively and respond promptly to the most severe threats, organizations can use the "sort" command to prioritize security incidents based on factors such as impact severity and potential business impact, incident containment and eradication are essential components that focus on stopping the spread of the incident and removing the root cause from the affected systems, containment measures may include isolating compromised systems from the network, blocking malicious communication channels, or disabling compromised user accounts, organizations can use the "netstat" command to identify active network connections and the "kill" command to terminate suspicious processes, eradication efforts typically involve removing malware, patching vulnerabilities, and restoring affected systems to a known good state, organizations can use the "apt-get" command to install security updates and patches, incident recovery is another critical component that focuses on restoring normal operations and data integrity after an incident, recovery measures may include restoring data from backups, rebuilding compromised systems, and implementing additional security controls to prevent similar incidents in the future, organizations can use the "rsync" command to synchronize data between backup servers and production systems, finally, post-incident analysis and lessons learned are essential components that involve conducting a thorough review of the incident response process to identify areas for improvement and implement corrective actions, organizations can use the "grep" command to search for specific incident-related events in log files and analyze the root causes of security incidents, overall, these key components form the foundation of an effective incident response program, enabling organizations to detect, respond to, and recover from cybersecurity incidents in a timely and efficient manner.

Chapter 2: Developing an Incident Response Plan

Designing an effective incident response plan is crucial for organizations to mitigate the impact of cybersecurity incidents and minimize potential damage to their assets and operations, an incident response plan outlines the steps and procedures that the organization will follow when responding to security incidents, the first step in designing an incident response plan is to establish clear objectives and goals, organizations should define the scope of the plan, identify the types of incidents it will address, and establish roles and responsibilities for key stakeholders, this can be achieved using the "vim" or "nano" command to create a text file outlining the objectives and goals of the incident response plan, once objectives and goals are defined, organizations should conduct a risk assessment to identify potential threats and vulnerabilities that could lead to security incidents, a risk assessment helps prioritize resources and focus efforts on addressing the most critical risks, organizations can use tools such as vulnerability scanners and risk assessment frameworks to identify and prioritize security risks, such as "nmap" for network scanning and "OpenVAS" for vulnerability assessment, after identifying risks, organizations should develop incident response procedures to address each type of security incident, procedures should outline the steps to take when responding to incidents, including how to detect, contain, eradicate, and recover from security breaches, procedures should be clear, concise, and easy to follow, organizations can use the "vim" or "nano" command to create a text file outlining incident response procedures, including step-by-step instructions and command-line commands, once procedures are defined, organizations should establish communication and coordination mechanisms to ensure effective collaboration between internal teams and external stakeholders during incident response efforts, this may include setting up communication channels such as email distribution lists, phone trees, and incident response communication tools, organizations can use the "mail" command to send email notifications to incident response team members and stakeholders, and the "curl" command to integrate with incident response communication platforms, such as Slack or Microsoft Teams, in addition to communication mechanisms, organizations should establish incident response workflows to streamline the response process and ensure that all necessary steps are followed, workflows define the sequence of actions to be taken during incident response and specify the roles and responsibilities of each team member, organizations can use tools such as workflow management software or project management platforms to create and automate incident response workflows, such as "Jira" or "Trello", once the incident response plan is designed, organizations should regularly test and update the plan to ensure its effectiveness and relevance, this includes conducting tabletop exercises, simulated incident scenarios, and post-incident reviews to identify areas for improvement and refine response procedures, organizations can use tools such as "Metasploit" or "OWASP ZAP" to simulate cyber attacks and test the effectiveness of their incident response plan, overall, designing an effective incident response plan is essential for organizations to effectively detect, respond to, and recover from cybersecurity incidents, it helps minimize the impact of incidents and ensure business continuity in the face of evolving threats. Roles and responsibilities in incident response are crucial for ensuring effective coordination and collaboration during security incidents, each team member plays a specific role and has defined responsibilities to contribute to the overall incident response effort, one of the key roles in incident response is that of the incident response coordinator, who is responsible for overseeing the entire incident response process and coordinating the efforts of all team members, the incident response coordinator is typically a senior member of the organization's security team and serves as the primary point of contact for communicating with stakeholders, another important role is that of the incident responder, who is responsible for executing the incident response plan and carrying out specific tasks to contain and mitigate security incidents, incident responders are often divided into specialized teams, such as network security, endpoint security, and forensics, each team focuses on a specific aspect of incident response, such as identifying and containing malware infections or analyzing network traffic for signs of unauthorized access, within each team, there may be further roles and responsibilities assigned to individual team members, for example, in a network security team, there may be roles such as network analyst, firewall administrator, and intrusion detection specialist, each responsible for specific tasks related to monitoring and securing the organization's network infrastructure, incident response teams also work closely with other internal teams, such as IT operations, legal, and communications, to ensure a coordinated response to security incidents, IT operations teams may be responsible for implementing technical controls to contain and remediate security threats, while legal teams may provide guidance on compliance requirements and legal obligations, communications teams are responsible for managing internal and external communications during security incidents, ensuring that stakeholders are kept informed and that the organization's reputation is protected, incident response teams may also work with external stakeholders, such as law enforcement agencies, regulatory bodies, and third-party vendors, depending on the nature and severity of the incident, each stakeholder has a role to play in the incident response process, and it is important for incident response teams to establish clear lines of communication and collaboration with all stakeholders, incident response plans should clearly define roles and responsibilities for each team member and stakeholder, outlining their specific tasks and duties during security incidents, this helps ensure that everyone knows what is expected of them and can respond effectively to incidents when they occur, regular training and exercises are also essential for ensuring that team members are prepared to fulfill their roles and responsibilities during real-world incidents, training helps familiarize team members with the incident response plan, tools, and procedures, while exercises provide an opportunity to practice and refine incident response skills in a simulated environment, overall, roles and responsibilities are fundamental to the success of incident response efforts, ensuring that everyone knows what they need to do and can work together effectively to detect, respond to, and recover from security incidents.

Chapter 3: Incident Triage and Prioritization

Prioritizing incidents based on severity is a critical aspect of incident response, as it helps organizations allocate resources effectively and focus on addressing the most significant threats first, severity is typically determined based on the potential impact of an incident on the organization's operations, assets, and reputation, as well as the likelihood of the incident occurring, incidents that pose a high risk to critical systems, sensitive data, or regulatory compliance are usually prioritized as high severity, while incidents with minimal impact or low likelihood may be classified as low severity, one common method for prioritizing incidents is to use a severity matrix, which assigns a severity level to each incident based on predefined criteria, such as the type of data involved, the number of systems affected, and the duration of the incident, severity matrices can help incident responders quickly assess the potential impact of an incident and prioritize their response accordingly, for example, a severity matrix may classify a data breach involving personally identifiable information (PII) as high severity, while a minor service disruption may be classified as low severity, incident response teams may also use incident classification frameworks, such as the Common Vulnerability Scoring System (CVSS), to prioritize incidents, CVSS assigns a numerical score to each vulnerability based on its severity, exploitability, and impact, allowing organizations to prioritize their response efforts based on the overall risk posed by each vulnerability, incident response teams should also consider other factors when prioritizing incidents, such as the organization's business objectives, regulatory requirements, and available resources, for example, an incident that threatens to disrupt critical business operations may be prioritized over a less critical incident, even if it has a lower severity rating, incident prioritization should be a collaborative process involving key stakeholders from across the organization, including IT, security, legal, and business units, these stakeholders can provide valuable input on the potential impact of an incident and help ensure that response efforts are aligned with the organization's strategic objectives, once incidents have been prioritized, incident response teams can develop and implement response plans tailored to the severity of each incident, for high severity incidents, response plans may include activating an incident response team, notifying senior management and legal counsel, and coordinating with external stakeholders, such as law enforcement and regulatory agencies, for low severity incidents, response plans may be less formal and may focus on containment and remediation efforts, incident response teams should regularly review and update their incident prioritization criteria to ensure that they remain relevant and effective, this may involve incorporating lessons learned from previous incidents, changes in the threat landscape, and updates to regulatory requirements, by prioritizing incidents based on severity, organizations can focus their resources on addressing the most significant threats first, minimizing the impact of security incidents, and protecting the organization's assets and reputation. Incident triage techniques and tools are essential components of effective incident response processes, enabling organizations to quickly assess and prioritize incoming security incidents, incident triage involves the initial assessment of an incident to determine its severity, scope, and potential impact, as well as the appropriate response actions, one common technique used in incident triage is the use of triage matrices or decision trees, which provide a structured framework for evaluating incidents based on predefined criteria, such as the type of incident, the systems or data affected, and the potential business impact, incident response teams can use these matrices to classify incidents into different categories, such as high, medium, or low severity, based on their assessment of the incident's characteristics, incident response teams may also use automated triage tools to streamline the incident assessment process, these tools can automatically collect and analyze relevant data from security alerts, logs, and other sources to identify potential security incidents, some examples of popular incident triage tools include Splunk, IBM QRadar, and Elastic Security, these tools use advanced analytics and machine learning algorithms to prioritize incidents based on their severity and potential impact, incident response teams can then use this information to allocate resources more effectively and focus on addressing the most critical threats first, in addition to automated triage tools, incident response teams may also use manual triage techniques, such as checklists and decision trees, to assess security incidents, these techniques involve gathering information about the incident, analyzing it to determine its severity and scope, and then selecting the appropriate response actions, incident response teams may also use command-line tools to gather additional information about security incidents and assess their severity, for example, the "netstat" command can be used to view active network connections and identify any suspicious or unauthorized activity, while the "ps" command can be used to list running processes and identify any malicious or suspicious processes, incident response teams may also use forensic analysis tools, such as the Sleuth Kit and Autopsy, to analyze disk images and memory dumps for evidence of security incidents, these tools can help incident responders identify indicators of compromise (IOCs), such as malware files, suspicious network connections, and unauthorized access attempts, incident triage is a critical step in the incident response process, as it allows organizations to quickly assess incoming security incidents and prioritize their response efforts, by using a combination of automated and manual triage techniques and tools, incident response teams can effectively manage security incidents and minimize their impact on the organization's operations and assets.

Chapter 4: Initial Response and Containment Strategies

Immediate response actions in incident handling are crucial for minimizing the impact of security incidents and restoring the affected systems to a secure state, these actions typically involve containing the incident, preserving evidence, and mitigating further damage, one of the first steps in incident response is to contain the incident to prevent it from spreading and causing additional harm, this can involve isolating affected systems from the network, disabling compromised user accounts, or blocking malicious network traffic, for example, in the case of a malware infection, network administrators may use firewall rules or network access control lists (ACLs) to block communication between infected and uninfected systems, or they may use host-based firewall software to restrict the malware's ability to communicate over the network, containment actions should be taken as quickly as possible to limit the impact of the incident and prevent further damage, once the incident has been contained, it's important to preserve evidence for further investigation and analysis, this may involve taking forensic images of affected systems, capturing network traffic, or logging relevant information such as timestamps, IP addresses, and user activity, forensic imaging tools such as FTK Imager or dd can be used to create bit-by-bit copies of hard drives or other storage devices, while network packet capture tools such as Wireshark or tcpdump can be used to capture and analyze network traffic, preserving evidence ensures that investigators have access to the information they need to understand the scope and impact of the incident, as well as to identify the root cause and any vulnerabilities that may have been exploited, while containment and evidence preservation are important immediate response actions, it's also essential to mitigate the immediate risks posed by the incident, this may involve removing malware from infected systems, restoring data from backups, or implementing temporary workarounds to restore critical services, for example, in the case of a ransomware attack, organizations may choose to restore affected systems from backups rather than paying the ransom, or they may implement temporary measures such as disabling remote access to critical systems until the incident has been fully resolved, mitigating the immediate risks of an incident helps to minimize its impact on the organization's operations and assets, as well as to restore normal business operations as quickly as possible, incident handlers should also communicate with relevant stakeholders, including senior management, legal counsel, and law enforcement, to keep them informed about the incident and its potential impact, this may involve drafting incident reports, coordinating with external parties such as forensic investigators or incident response consultants, or providing updates to affected users and customers, effective communication is essential for maintaining transparency and trust during an incident and ensuring that all stakeholders are aligned on the response strategy and next steps, overall, immediate response actions are critical for effective incident handling, by quickly containing the incident, preserving evidence, mitigating further damage, and communicating with stakeholders, incident handlers can minimize the impact of security incidents and restore normal operations as quickly as possible. Containment strategies for incident mitigation are essential components of effective incident response plans, designed to minimize the impact of security incidents and prevent further damage to organizational assets, these strategies involve isolating affected systems, networks, or applications to prevent the spread of malicious activity, containing an incident promptly is crucial to limit its scope and prevent it from escalating into a larger-scale security breach, one common containment strategy is network segmentation, which involves dividing a network into separate segments or subnets and implementing access controls to restrict communication between them, this can help prevent the lateral movement of attackers within the network and contain the impact of a compromised system, for example, network administrators can use VLANs (Virtual Local Area Networks) to separate different departments or types of systems, such as servers, workstations, and IoT devices, and apply firewall rules or ACLs (Access Control Lists) to control traffic between VLANs, another containment strategy is the use of firewalls and intrusion detection/prevention systems (IDS/IPS) to block or monitor suspicious network traffic, firewalls can be configured to block known malicious IP addresses, domains, or protocols, while IDS/IPS systems can detect and alert on suspicious activity, such as port scans, brute-force attacks, or unauthorized access attempts, in addition to network-based containment strategies, organizations can also implement host-based containment measures to isolate compromised systems and prevent them from interacting with other systems or services, this can involve disabling unnecessary services, blocking unauthorized processes or applications, or disconnecting infected systems from the network, for example, system administrators can use the "iptables" command on Linux systems to create firewall rules to block specific network traffic or the "netsh advfirewall" command on Windows systems to configure Windows Firewall settings, containment strategies should be tailored to the specific incident and the organization's environment, considering factors such as the nature of the attack, the type of systems or data affected, and the potential impact on business operations, for example, in the case of a malware outbreak, containment measures may involve isolating infected systems, blocking malicious domains or IP addresses, and restricting access to sensitive data or critical systems, it's also important to consider the potential impact of containment measures on business operations and to balance security requirements with the need to maintain productivity, for example, while isolating infected systems may prevent the spread of malware, it may also disrupt normal business activities and require alternative arrangements to ensure continuity of operations, throughout the containment process, incident responders should continuously monitor the effectiveness of containment measures and adjust their approach as needed based on new information or changes in the threat landscape, this may involve analyzing network traffic, reviewing logs and alerts, or conducting forensic analysis to identify additional indicators of compromise or attack vectors, by implementing effective containment strategies, organizations can minimize the impact of security incidents, prevent further damage to their assets, and facilitate the recovery and restoration of normal business operations.

Chapter 5: Forensic Analysis Techniques

Digital forensics fundamentals encompass a broad range of techniques and methodologies used to investigate and analyze digital evidence in support of legal proceedings or incident response activities, these fundamentals are rooted in principles of data integrity, chain of custody, and the scientific method, digital forensics involves the identification, preservation, analysis, and presentation of electronic evidence, which can include data stored on computers, mobile devices, network servers, and other digital media, the goal of digital forensics is to reconstruct events, uncover the truth, and provide reliable evidence for use in court or other legal proceedings, forensic investigations often begin with the identification and preservation of evidence to ensure its integrity and admissibility in court, this typically involves creating a forensic image or copy of the original storage media, such as a hard drive or memory card, using specialized tools and techniques to prevent alteration or contamination of the evidence, one commonly used command for creating a forensic image is "dd" in Linux, which can be used to create a bit-by-bit copy of a disk or partition, for example, to create a forensic image of a disk named "/dev/sda" and save it to a file named "evidence.dd", the command would be "dd if=/dev/sda of=evidence.dd bs=4M", once the evidence is preserved, forensic analysts can proceed with the analysis phase, which involves examining the contents of the forensic image to extract relevant information and identify potential artifacts or indicators of suspicious activity, this can include recovering deleted files, examining file metadata, analyzing network traffic logs, and searching for evidence of malware or unauthorized access, forensic analysis tools such as Autopsy, Sleuth Kit, and EnCase are commonly used to assist with this process, these tools provide features for keyword searching, file carving, timeline analysis, and other forensic techniques, enabling analysts to uncover hidden or deleted data and reconstruct the sequence of events, during the analysis phase, forensic examiners must adhere to strict guidelines and procedures to ensure the integrity and reliability of their findings, this includes documenting their actions, maintaining a detailed chain of custody for all evidence, and following established forensic methodologies and best practices, once the analysis is complete, the findings are typically documented in a forensic report, which summarizes the results of the investigation, identifies key findings, and provides supporting evidence for each conclusion, the forensic report may also include recommendations for further action, such as legal proceedings or remediation steps to address security vulnerabilities or prevent future incidents, in addition to supporting legal proceedings, digital forensics plays a critical role in incident response and cybersecurity investigations, helping organizations identify the source and scope of security incidents, assess the impact on their systems and data, and develop effective response strategies, by leveraging digital forensics fundamentals and techniques, organizations can improve their ability to detect, respond to, and recover from security breaches, thereby enhancing their overall cybersecurity posture and protecting against future threats. Forensic analysis tools and methodologies encompass a diverse range of techniques and software applications used to investigate digital evidence and analyze forensic artifacts, these tools are essential for forensic examiners and investigators to effectively collect, preserve, and analyze data from various digital sources, including computers, mobile devices, network servers, and cloud environments, the use of forensic analysis tools is guided by established methodologies and best practices to ensure the integrity and admissibility of the evidence in legal proceedings, one widely used forensic analysis tool is Autopsy, an open-source digital forensics platform that provides a graphical interface for conducting forensic examinations, Autopsy supports the analysis of disk images, file systems, and network packet captures, allowing examiners to search for files, extract metadata, and recover deleted data, another popular tool is The Sleuth Kit (TSK), which is a collection of command-line utilities for analyzing disk images and file systems, TSK provides capabilities for file system analysis, timeline reconstruction, and keyword searching, making it a valuable tool for forensic investigations, to use TSK to analyze a disk image named "evidence.dd" and display information about the partitions, the command "mmls evidence.dd" can be executed, this will show the layout of the disk image and the offsets of each partition, digital forensics examiners also rely on specialized tools for extracting and analyzing data from mobile devices, one such tool is Cellebrite UFED (Universal Forensic Extraction Device), which is designed to acquire data from smartphones, tablets, and other mobile devices, UFED supports a wide range of device models and operating systems, allowing examiners to extract call logs, text messages, images, and other types of data for analysis, to use UFED to acquire data from an Android device connected via USB, the "ufed" command can be executed, this will initiate the acquisition process and create a forensic image of the device's storage, in addition to commercial tools, there are also open-source forensic analysis tools available, such as Volatility, which is a memory forensics framework used to analyze volatile memory (RAM) dumps, Volatility provides capabilities for examining running processes, network connections, and loaded kernel modules, making it a valuable tool for investigating malware infections and other security incidents, to analyze a memory dump named "memdump.raw" using Volatility and display information about running processes, the command "volatility -f memdump.raw pslist" can be executed, this will show a list of processes extracted from the memory dump, digital forensics tools are often used in combination with established methodologies and procedures to ensure thorough and accurate analysis of digital evidence, this includes following a systematic approach to evidence collection, preservation, and analysis, as well as documenting findings and maintaining a detailed chain of custody for all evidence, by leveraging forensic analysis tools and methodologies, forensic examiners and investigators can uncover valuable insights from digital evidence, helping to identify the cause of security incidents, attribute attacks to specific threat actors, and support legal proceedings with reliable and admissible evidence.

Chapter 6: Malware Analysis and Reverse Engineering

Malware analysis approaches encompass a variety of techniques and methodologies used to dissect and understand malicious software, these approaches are essential for cybersecurity professionals to identify the behavior, functionality, and impact of malware on computer systems, networks, and applications, one common approach to malware analysis is static analysis, which involves examining the code and structure of a malware sample without executing it, static analysis techniques include examining file headers, disassembling executable files, and analyzing strings and embedded resources, these techniques can reveal valuable information about the malware's functionality, such as its file format, import/export functions, and API calls, to perform static analysis on a Windows executable file named "malware.exe," the "objdump" command can be used to disassemble the binary code and display the assembly instructions, this will provide insights into the malware's logic and behavior, another approach to malware analysis is dynamic analysis, which involves executing the malware in a controlled environment, such as a virtual machine or sandbox, to observe its behavior and interactions with the system, dynamic analysis techniques include monitoring system calls, network traffic, and file system activity generated by the malware, these techniques can help identify malicious behaviors, such as file encryption, network communication, and process injection, to perform dynamic analysis on a malware sample in a virtual machine environment, tools such as Cuckoo Sandbox can be used to execute the malware and capture its behavior, Cuckoo Sandbox provides capabilities for analyzing malware behavior, generating reports, and extracting indicators of compromise (IOCs), such as file hashes, IP addresses, and domain names, in addition to static and dynamic analysis, malware analysts also employ other techniques, such as memory analysis, code emulation, and reverse engineering, to gain deeper insights into the behavior and capabilities of malware, memory analysis involves examining the contents of a system's memory (RAM) to identify running processes, loaded modules, and artifacts left by malware, tools such as Volatility can be used to perform memory analysis and extract forensic artifacts from memory dumps, code emulation involves running malware samples in a virtualized environment to analyze their behavior without executing them on a real system, tools such as QEMU and VMware can be used to create virtualized environments for malware analysis, reverse engineering involves analyzing the binary code of malware to understand its functionality and identify vulnerabilities, tools such as IDA Pro and Radare2 can be used to disassemble and analyze malware binaries, by employing a combination of static, dynamic, and other analysis techniques, malware analysts can gain a comprehensive understanding of malware behavior, enabling them to develop effective countermeasures and defenses against cyber threats. Reverse engineering malicious code is a crucial skill in cybersecurity, allowing analysts to understand the inner workings of malware and develop effective countermeasures, this process involves analyzing malware binaries to uncover their functionality, evasion techniques, and potential vulnerabilities, to begin reverse engineering a malicious binary, analysts typically start by obtaining a copy of the malware sample, which can be acquired from various sources, such as malware repositories, honeypots, or incident response investigations, once the malware sample is obtained, analysts use specialized tools and techniques to analyze its behavior and structure, one common tool used in reverse engineering is a disassembler, such as IDA Pro or Ghidra, which allows analysts to view the assembly code of the malware and navigate its control flow, another useful tool is a debugger, such as OllyDbg or WinDbg, which enables analysts to dynamically analyze the malware's execution and inspect its memory and registers, to begin reverse engineering a malware sample using IDA Pro, analysts can open the binary file in the IDA Pro interface and start analyzing its code and functions, this process involves navigating through the disassembled code, identifying function calls, and understanding the malware's control flow, analysts can also use IDA Pro's interactive features, such as graph view and cross-references, to visualize the code structure and relationships between different functions, in addition to disassembly and debugging tools, analysts may also use other techniques, such as code deobfuscation, string analysis, and pattern recognition, to uncover the malware's functionality and intent, code deobfuscation involves reversing the obfuscation techniques used by malware authors to hide their code and evade detection, string analysis involves extracting and analyzing strings embedded in the malware binary, such as URLs, domain names, and command-and-control (C2) server addresses, pattern recognition involves identifying common patterns and signatures in the malware code, such as encryption algorithms, API calls, and code injection techniques, by applying these techniques in combination with disassembly and debugging tools, analysts can gain valuable insights into the behavior and capabilities of the malware, allowing them to develop effective countermeasures and defenses, however, reverse engineering malicious code can be a complex and time-consuming process, requiring specialized skills and expertise, analysts must be familiar with assembly language, binary analysis, and malware evasion techniques to effectively reverse engineer malware, they must also stay updated on the latest trends and developments in malware analysis and reverse engineering, as malware authors constantly evolve their tactics and techniques to evade detection and analysis, overall, reverse engineering malicious code is an essential skill for cybersecurity professionals, enabling them to analyze and understand the behavior of malware and develop effective strategies to detect, mitigate, and prevent cyber threats.

Chapter 7: Network Traffic Analysis in Incident Response

Network traffic analysis is a crucial aspect of cybersecurity, allowing organizations to monitor and understand the flow of data within their networks, this process involves capturing, inspecting, and analyzing network traffic to detect suspicious activities, identify security threats, and investigate security incidents, by analyzing network traffic, organizations can gain valuable insights into the behavior of users, devices, and applications on their networks, enabling them to identify abnormal patterns, anomalies, and potential security breaches, network traffic analysis plays a vital role in threat detection and prevention, helping organizations to detect and mitigate various cyber threats, such as malware infections, data breaches, insider threats, and network intrusions, one of the key benefits of network traffic analysis is its ability to provide real-time visibility into network activity, allowing organizations to monitor and respond to security events as they occur, this proactive approach to security enables organizations to detect and block threats before they can cause significant damage, network traffic analysis also helps organizations to

274

identify unauthorized or malicious activities on their networks, such as unauthorized access attempts, data exfiltration, and command-and-control communications, by monitoring network traffic, organizations can detect these activities and take immediate action to prevent further harm, another important aspect of network traffic analysis is its role in incident response and forensic investigations, when a security incident occurs, analysts can use network traffic analysis to reconstruct the timeline of events, identify the source of the attack, and determine the extent of the compromise, this information is critical for understanding how the attack occurred and developing effective response strategies, to perform network traffic analysis, organizations can use a variety of tools and techniques, one common tool used for network traffic analysis is a network packet analyzer, such as Wireshark or tcpdump, which allows analysts to capture and inspect network packets in real-time, these tools provide detailed information about network traffic, including source and destination IP addresses, protocols, ports, and packet payloads, analysts can use this information to identify suspicious or malicious traffic and investigate security incidents, in addition to packet analyzers, organizations can also use network intrusion detection systems (NIDS) and network intrusion prevention systems (NIPS) to monitor and analyze network traffic for signs of suspicious activity, these systems use a combination of signature-based and behavior-based detection techniques to identify and block potential threats, organizations can also leverage log data from network devices, such as firewalls, routers, and switches, to perform network traffic analysis, these logs contain valuable information about network activity, including connection logs, access logs, and security logs, by aggregating and analyzing this log data, organizations can gain a comprehensive view of network traffic and identify potential security issues, overall, network traffic analysis is a critical component of cybersecurity, providing organizations with the visibility and insights they need to detect, prevent, and respond to cyber threats effectively. Network forensics refers to the process of investigating and analyzing network traffic to gather evidence and determine the cause of security incidents or breaches, this discipline plays a crucial role in incident response, legal proceedings, and cybersecurity investigations, network forensics tools and techniques enable investigators to capture, inspect, and analyze network packets to reconstruct the timeline of events, identify malicious activities, and attribute security incidents to specific individuals or entities, these tools and techniques help organizations to understand how security breaches occurred, identify the scope of the compromise, and develop effective response strategies, one commonly used tool for network forensics is a network packet capture tool, such as Wireshark or tcpdump, these tools allow investigators to capture and store network packets in real-time or from packet capture files for later analysis, investigators can use these tools to filter, search, and analyze captured packets to extract valuable information about network activity, another important aspect of network forensics is the analysis of network logs, network devices such as firewalls, routers, and switches generate log data that contains information about network traffic, connections, and security events, investigators can use log analysis tools and techniques to review and analyze this data to identify suspicious activities, detect security breaches, and reconstruct the sequence of events, in addition to packet capture and log analysis, network forensics also involves the analysis of network protocols and traffic patterns, investigators can examine the characteristics of network traffic, such as protocol usage, packet sizes, and communication patterns, to identify anomalies and potential security threats, network forensics tools often include features for protocol analysis and traffic pattern analysis to assist investigators in this process, network forensics also involves the use of advanced techniques such as deep packet inspection (DPI) and flow analysis, deep packet inspection allows investigators to inspect the contents of network packets at a granular level to identify malicious payloads, exploits, and other indicators of compromise, flow analysis involves the analysis of network flow data to identify patterns of communication, detect abnormal behavior, and detect security incidents, network forensics tools may include DPI and flow analysis capabilities to help investigators gain deeper insights into network activity, in addition to these technical tools and techniques, network forensics also requires a solid understanding of networking protocols, security principles, and investigative methodologies, investigators must be able to interpret the results of their analysis accurately and effectively communicate their findings to stakeholders, this requires strong analytical skills, attention to detail, and knowledge of cybersecurity best practices, in summary, network forensics tools and techniques are essential for investigating and analyzing security incidents, these tools enable investigators to capture, analyze, and interpret network traffic to gather evidence, identify security threats, and attribute security incidents, by leveraging these tools and techniques, organizations can enhance their ability to detect, respond to, and mitigate cyber threats effectively.

Chapter 8: Endpoint Detection and Response (EDR)

Endpoint security refers to the strategies and technologies deployed to protect the endpoints of a network, including desktops, laptops, servers, and mobile devices, these endpoints are often targeted by cyber attackers as points of entry into a network, making endpoint security a critical component of any cybersecurity program, traditional antivirus solutions are no longer sufficient to protect against modern threats, such as advanced malware, ransomware, and zero-day exploits, as a result, organizations are adopting more advanced endpoint security solutions that offer a range of detection and prevention capabilities, one key capability of modern endpoint security solutions is endpoint detection and response (EDR), EDR solutions provide real-time visibility into endpoint activity and behavior, allowing organizations to detect and respond to threats more effectively, EDR solutions collect telemetry data from endpoints, such as process execution, file system activity, and network connections, and analyze this data to identify suspicious behavior and indicators of compromise, many EDR solutions also include features for automated response and threat hunting, enabling organizations to proactively identify and mitigate threats, another important capability of endpoint security solutions is application control, application control allows organizations to control which applications are allowed to run on endpoints, helping to prevent unauthorized software from executing and reducing the risk of malware infections, application control solutions use whitelisting and blacklisting techniques to enforce security policies and block malicious software, organizations can deploy application control solutions using Group Policy in Windows environments or through third-party endpoint security platforms, such as CrowdStrike Falcon or Carbon Black, next-generation antivirus (NGAV) is another key component of modern endpoint security solutions, NGAV solutions use advanced machine learning and behavioral analysis techniques to detect and block malware in real-time, NGAV solutions are designed to be more effective than traditional signature-based antivirus solutions at detecting unknown and zero-day threats, organizations can deploy

NGAV solutions alongside EDR solutions for comprehensive endpoint protection, network-based detection capabilities are also important for endpoint security, many attacks originate from the network and spread to endpoints, so organizations need to be able to detect and block malicious network traffic before it reaches endpoints, intrusion detection and prevention systems (IDPS) and network traffic analysis (NTA) solutions can help organizations to monitor network traffic for signs of malicious activity and respond to threats in real-time, IDPS solutions can detect and block known attacks based on signatures and behavioral analysis, while NTA solutions use machine learning and anomaly detection techniques to identify abnormal network behavior, organizations can deploy IDPS and NTA solutions at network chokepoints, such as perimeter firewalls and internal network segments, to protect endpoints from network-based attacks, in addition to these detection capabilities, endpoint security solutions also include features for vulnerability management, patch management, and device control, vulnerability management solutions scan endpoints for known vulnerabilities and prioritize remediation based on risk, patch management solutions automate the process of applying security patches to endpoints to reduce the risk of exploitation, and device control solutions enforce security policies to control the use of removable storage devices, mobile devices, and other endpoints, organizations can deploy these capabilities as part of an integrated endpoint security platform or as standalone solutions, depending on their specific requirements and budget, In summary, endpoint security is a critical component of any cybersecurity program, organizations need to deploy advanced endpoint security solutions that offer a range of detection and prevention capabilities to protect against modern threats, including EDR, application control, NGAV, network-based detection, vulnerability management, patch management, and device control, by deploying these capabilities, organizations can better protect their endpoints from cyber attacks and reduce the risk of data breaches and other security incidents. Leveraging Endpoint Detection and Response (EDR) solutions for incident response is a crucial aspect of modern cybersecurity practices, EDR solutions provide organizations with real-time visibility into endpoint activity and behavior, allowing them to detect and respond to security incidents more effectively, when an incident occurs, EDR solutions enable security teams to quickly investigate the scope and impact of the incident, one of the key features of EDR solutions is the ability to collect telemetry data from endpoints, including process execution, file system activity, and network connections, this data provides valuable insights into the behavior of endpoints and helps security teams to identify and prioritize incidents, to leverage EDR solutions for incident response, security teams must first ensure that the EDR solution is properly deployed and configured across their endpoints, this typically involves deploying an agent on each endpoint and configuring the EDR solution to collect the necessary telemetry data, once the EDR solution is deployed, security teams can use it to monitor endpoints for signs of suspicious activity, in the event of an incident, security teams can use the EDR solution to quickly investigate the incident and determine the root cause, for example, security teams can use the EDR solution to identify the process that initiated the incident and trace its activity across endpoints, this level of visibility is crucial for understanding the scope of the incident and developing an effective response strategy, in addition to investigation capabilities, EDR solutions also include features for automated response, these features allow security teams to automatically contain and remediate incidents in real-time, for example, security teams can use the EDR solution to isolate an infected endpoint from the network or terminate a malicious process, this helps to minimize the impact of the incident and prevent it from spreading to other endpoints, another key aspect of leveraging EDR solutions for incident response is threat hunting, threat hunting involves proactively searching for signs of compromise and indicators of attack across endpoints, security teams can use the EDR solution to perform threat hunting activities, such as searching for suspicious files or analyzing anomalous behavior, this helps to identify and mitigate threats before they escalate into full-blown incidents, to make the most of EDR solutions for incident response, organizations should integrate their EDR solution with other security tools and technologies, for example, organizations can integrate their EDR solution with their Security Information and Event Management (SIEM) system to correlate endpoint telemetry data with other security events and alerts, this provides security teams with a more comprehensive view of their security posture and helps them to prioritize incidents more effectively, overall, leveraging EDR solutions for incident response is essential for organizations looking to enhance their cybersecurity capabilities and protect against advanced threats, by deploying and properly configuring EDR solutions, organizations can improve their ability to detect, investigate, and respond to security incidents in real-time, this helps to minimize the impact of incidents and reduce the risk of data breaches and other security breaches.

Chapter 9: Advanced Incident Response Techniques

Advanced incident handling strategies are essential components of a robust cybersecurity posture, these strategies go beyond the basics of incident response and focus on proactive measures to prevent and mitigate security incidents, one advanced strategy is to establish an incident response team (IRT) comprised of skilled professionals from various disciplines, such as network security, forensics, and legal, this team is responsible for coordinating and executing the organization's incident response efforts, including threat detection, analysis, and containment, establishing an IRT involves defining roles and responsibilities, developing policies and procedures, and conducting regular training and drills to ensure readiness, another advanced strategy is to implement a threat intelligence program, threat intelligence provides valuable insights into emerging threats, attack trends, and adversary tactics, organizations can leverage threat intelligence to enhance their incident detection capabilities and improve their response effectiveness, threat intelligence sources include open-source intelligence (OSINT), commercial threat feeds, and information sharing partnerships, organizations can use threat intelligence to identify indicators of compromise (IOCs), such as malicious IP addresses, domains, and file hashes, and proactively block or mitigate threats before they cause harm, automation is another key component of advanced incident handling strategies, automation enables organizations to streamline repetitive tasks, accelerate incident response times, and reduce human error, common automation tasks include threat detection, alert triage, and incident enrichment, organizations can use security orchestration, automation, and response (SOAR) platforms to automate incident response workflows and integrate with other security tools and systems, this allows for faster and more efficient incident detection, investigation, and remediation, another advanced strategy is to implement a proactive threat hunting program, threat hunting involves actively searching for signs of compromise and attacker activity within an organization's environment, rather than waiting for alerts or incidents to occur, threat hunters use a combination of tools, techniques, and expertise to uncover hidden threats and vulnerabilities, organizations can leverage threat hunting to identify and mitigate threats before they escalate into full-blown incidents, effective threat hunting requires a deep understanding of the organization's environment, attacker behavior, and common attack techniques, as well as access to high-quality data and advanced analytics tools, incident response orchestration is another advanced strategy that organizations can use to streamline their incident handling processes, incident response orchestration involves automating the coordination and execution of incident response tasks across multiple teams and technologies, this helps to ensure a consistent and efficient response to security incidents, organizations can use incident response orchestration platforms to define and automate response playbooks, which outline the steps to be taken in response to different types of incidents, these playbooks can include a combination of manual and automated tasks, such as gathering threat intelligence, isolating infected systems, and notifying stakeholders, incident response orchestration platforms also provide visibility and control over the incident response process, allowing organizations to track the status of incidents, assign tasks to team members, and generate reports for management and compliance purposes, overall, advanced incident handling strategies are essential for organizations looking to effectively detect, respond to, and recover from security incidents, by implementing proactive measures, leveraging threat intelligence, automating response workflows, and orchestrating incident response efforts, organizations can better protect their assets, mitigate risk, and maintain business continuity in the face of cyber threats. Incident response automation and orchestration (IRAO) is a critical component of modern cybersecurity operations, it involves using technology to automate and streamline the process of detecting, analyzing, and responding to security incidents, IRAO platforms help organizations improve the efficiency and effectiveness of their incident response efforts by reducing manual intervention, accelerating response times, and ensuring consistency across the incident lifecycle, one of the key benefits of IRAO is its ability to handle the increasing volume and complexity of cyber threats faced by organizations, with the proliferation of sophisticated attacks and the growing attack surface, manual incident response processes are no longer sufficient to keep pace with the evolving threat landscape, IRAO enables organizations to scale their incident response capabilities to effectively address the growing number of security incidents, another benefit of IRAO is its ability to reduce response times and minimize the impact of security incidents, by automating repetitive tasks and orchestrating response actions, IRAO platforms enable organizations to detect and respond to threats more quickly, this is critical for minimizing the damage caused by cyber attacks and reducing the risk of data breaches, furthermore, IRAO helps organizations improve their incident response consistency and accuracy, by codifying response procedures into automated workflows, IRAO platforms ensure that response actions are executed in a standardized manner, this helps organizations maintain compliance with regulatory requirements and internal policies, as well as improve the overall effectiveness of their incident response efforts, IRAO platforms also enable organizations to leverage threat intelligence more effectively in their incident response processes, by integrating with threat intelligence feeds and security tools, IRAO platforms can automatically enrich incident data with relevant threat intelligence information, this helps analysts make more informed decisions and prioritize response efforts based on the severity and relevance of threats, moreover, IRAO platforms provide organizations with greater visibility and control over their incident response processes, by centralizing incident data and response workflows, IRAO platforms enable organizations to track the status of incidents in real-time, assign tasks to team members, and generate comprehensive reports for management and compliance purposes, this visibility helps organizations identify areas for improvement and optimize their incident response processes over time, in addition, IRAO platforms help organizations improve their incident response resilience and readiness, by automating routine tasks and response actions, IRAO platforms free up valuable time and resources that can be allocated to more strategic activities, such as threat hunting, vulnerability management, and security awareness training, this allows organizations to build more resilient security postures and better prepare for future cyber threats, furthermore, IRAO platforms enable organizations to adapt and respond more effectively to evolving threats and attack techniques, by integrating with security tools and technologies, IRAO platforms can automatically update response playbooks and workflows based on the latest threat intelligence and best practices, this helps organizations stay ahead of emerging threats and minimize their exposure to new vulnerabilities, overall, IRAO is a critical capability for organizations looking to enhance their cybersecurity posture and effectively defend against the growing number of cyber threats, by automating and orchestrating their incident response processes, organizations can improve their response times, reduce their risk exposure, and better protect their sensitive data and assets.

Chapter 10: Post-Incident Remediation and Lessons Learned

Post-Incident Recovery Processes are crucial components of any comprehensive incident response plan, they focus on restoring affected systems and services to their normal state following a security incident, these processes are essential for minimizing the impact of the incident and restoring the organization's operations to full functionality, post-incident recovery involves several key steps, including identifying and documenting the impact of the incident, assessing the damage to affected systems and data, and developing a plan for restoring operations, one of the first steps in post-incident recovery is to conduct a thorough assessment of the incident's impact, this involves identifying all systems and data that were affected by the incident, as well as determining the extent of the damage, organizations may use a variety of tools and techniques to assess the impact of an incident, including forensic analysis tools, log analysis, and interviews with affected personnel, once the impact of the incident has been assessed, the next step is to prioritize recovery efforts, organizations should prioritize the restoration of critical systems and data that are essential for business operations, this may involve restoring backups, rebuilding affected systems, or implementing temporary workarounds to maintain continuity of operations, organizations may also need to coordinate with external parties, such as vendors, customers, and regulatory agencies, to ensure a coordinated and effective recovery effort, depending on the nature and severity of the incident, organizations may need to implement additional security measures to prevent future incidents, this may include patching vulnerabilities, implementing new security controls, or conducting security awareness training for employees, throughout the post-incident recovery process, organizations should maintain clear communication with stakeholders, including employees, customers, and regulators, this helps to manage expectations and minimize the impact of the incident on the organization's reputation and business operations, organizations should also document all aspects of the post-incident recovery process, including the steps taken, the decisions made, and the lessons learned, this documentation can be used to improve the organization's incident response capabilities and inform future incident response planning efforts, finally, once the organization has fully recovered from the incident, it is important to conduct a post-incident review, this involves evaluating the organization's response to the incident, identifying areas for improvement, and implementing changes to strengthen the organization's incident response capabilities, by following these post-incident recovery processes, organizations can effectively recover from security incidents and minimize their impact on business operations and reputation. Conducting post-incident reviews and making improvements are critical aspects of an effective incident response process, these activities help organizations learn from security incidents and strengthen their security posture, a post-incident review involves analyzing the organization's response to an incident, identifying areas for improvement, and implementing changes to enhance incident response capabilities, one of the first steps in conducting a post-incident review is to gather relevant information about the incident, this may include incident reports, logs, communications records, and interviews with personnel involved in the response, organizations may use incident response management tools to collect and analyze this information, such as the Elastic Stack or Splunk, these tools allow organizations to search and visualize data related to the incident, enabling them to identify trends and patterns in the organization's response, once the relevant information has been collected, organizations can begin to assess the effectiveness of their response, this involves evaluating how well the organization followed its incident response plan, identified and contained the incident, communicated with stakeholders, and restored operations, organizations may use incident response metrics to measure the effectiveness of their response, such as mean time to detect (MTTD) and mean time to respond (MTTR), these metrics provide insights into how quickly the organization detected and responded to the incident, as well as how long it took to contain and remediate the incident, based on the findings of the post-incident review, organizations can identify areas for improvement in their incident response process, this may include updating the incident response plan, enhancing communication procedures, improving incident detection and containment capabilities, or providing additional training to incident response personnel, organizations should prioritize these improvements based on their potential impact on the organization's security posture and business operations, for example, if the post-incident review identifies a lack of visibility into the organization's network traffic as a contributing factor to the incident, the organization may prioritize implementing a network monitoring solution, such as Suricata or Zeek, to improve visibility and detection capabilities, once improvements have been identified, organizations should develop a plan to implement them, this plan should include specific tasks, timelines, and responsibilities for each improvement, organizations may also need to allocate resources, such as budget and personnel, to support the implementation of these improvements, throughout the implementation process, organizations should monitor progress and adjust their plans as needed, finally, after the improvements have been implemented, organizations should conduct follow-up assessments to ensure that the changes have been effective in strengthening the organization's incident response capabilities, this may involve conducting additional tests, such as tabletop exercises or red team assessments, to validate the improvements and identify any remaining gaps or weaknesses, by conducting post-incident reviews and making improvements based on the findings, organizations can continuously enhance their incident response capabilities and better protect against future security incidents.

Conclusion

In summary, the "CySA+ Study Guide: Exam CS0-003" bundle offers a comprehensive and structured approach to preparing for the CompTIA CySA+ certification exam. With four carefully curated books covering the foundational concepts of cybersecurity, vulnerability analysis, threat intelligence, and incident response, this bundle equips aspiring IT security professionals with the knowledge and skills needed to excel in their roles.

Book 1, "Foundations of Cybersecurity: A Beginner's Guide to CySA+ Exam CS0-003," lays the groundwork by providing an in-depth exploration of essential cybersecurity principles, including network security, cryptography, and access control. Readers will gain a solid understanding of core concepts, setting a strong foundation for their CySA+ journey.

Book 2, "Analyzing Vulnerabilities: Techniques and Tools for CySA+ Exam CS0-003," delves into the intricacies of vulnerability analysis, offering insights into various assessment techniques and tools used to identify and remediate security weaknesses. From vulnerability scanning to penetration testing, readers will learn how to assess and mitigate risks effectively.

Book 3, "Threat Intelligence Fundamentals: Advanced Strategies for CySA+ Exam CS0-003," takes a deep dive into the world of threat intelligence, exploring advanced strategies for gathering, analyzing, and leveraging threat intelligence to enhance security posture. Readers will learn how to proactively identify and respond to emerging threats, empowering them to stay one step ahead of adversaries.

Book 4, "Mastering Incident Response: Expert Tactics for CySA+ Exam CS0-003," rounds out the bundle by focusing on incident response, a critical aspect of cybersecurity operations. Readers will gain valuable insights into developing incident response plans, conducting post-incident analysis, and implementing effective response strategies to mitigate the impact of security incidents.

Together, these four books provide a comprehensive and cohesive study guide for the CySA+ certification exam, covering all domains and objectives outlined in the exam syllabus. Whether you're a novice cybersecurity professional looking to build a strong foundation or an experienced practitioner seeking to refine your skills, this bundle offers valuable insights and practical guidance to help you succeed in the dynamic field of IT security.

www.ingramcontent.com/pod-product-compliance
Lightning Source LLC
Chambersburg PA
CBHW071234050326
40690CB00011B/2110